GOD OF THE WHIRLWIND

HORROR, MEMORY, AND STORY IN BLACK WACO

EDITED BY TYLER B. DAVIS

FOREWORD BY STEVIE WALKER-WEBB

PHOTOGRAPHS BY MARK MENJÍVAR

1845 BOOKS

Cover and book design by Elyxandra Encarnación
Cover image: Mark Menjívar, "Washington Avenue Bridge"

Library of Congress Cataloging-in-Publication Data
Names: Davis, Tyler B., editor. | Menjívar, Mark, photographer. |
    Walker-Webb, Stevie, writer of foreword.
Title: God of the whirlwind: horror, memory, and story in Black Waco /
    Tyler B. Davis, editor; photographs by Mark Menjívar.
Description: Waco, Texas: 1845 Books, an imprint of Baylor University
    Press, [2024] | Includes bibliographical references and index. |
    Summary: "Chronicles how the memory of the 1953 Waco tornado has been
    interpreted through the lens of racial injustice among Black Wacoans"—
    Provided by publisher.
Identifiers: LCCN 2024044368 (print) | LCCN 2024044369 (ebook) | ISBN
    9781481322560 (paperback) | ISBN 9781481322577 (adobe pdf) | ISBN
    9781481322584 (epub)
Subjects: LCSH: Black people—Texas—Waco—History—20th century. | Black
    people—Texas—Waco—Social life and customs. | Waco (Tex.)—Race
    relations.
Classification: LCC E185.93.T4 D38 2024 (print) | LCC E185.93.T4 (ebook)
    | DDC 976.406—dc23/eng/20240930
LC record available at https://lccn.loc.gov/2024044368
LC ebook record available at https://lccn.loc.gov/2024044369

Although nothing is more certain than that memory fails,
equally, nothing is more certain than that
memory succeeds.

Karen E. Fields

Contents

List of Images   ix

Foreword by Stevie Walker-Webb   xi

Introduction by Tyler B. Davis   1

Part 1: Storm   15

1   LaRue Dorsey   21

2   Linda Jann Lewis   37

Part 2: Story   53

3   Michael D. Babers   59

4   Bettie V. Beard   69

5   Nona Kirkpatrick and Anthony Fulbright   85

Part 3: Spirit   97

6   Ramad D. Carter   103

7   George Oliver   117

8   Stevie Walker-Webb   131

Epilogue 139
The Spirit of the Whirlwind

Acknowledgments 143

Note on Editing Practices and Interviews 145

Notes 147

List of Images

Brazos River Sign   xiv

McLennan County Courthouse Rotunda   16

Detail of McLennan County Courthouse Rotunda   17

Doris Miller Memorial   18

McLennan County Courthouse   19

LaRue Dorsey   20

Linda Jann Lewis   36

Bridges over the Brazos River   54

Mural of the ALICO Building and Tornado   56

The ALICO Building, Downtown Waco   56

Kinetic Tornado Sculptures, Downtown Waco   57

The Waco Tornado Memorial   57

Reverend Michael D. Babers   58

Bettie V. Beard   68

Nona Kirkpatrick and Anthony Fulbright   84

Martin Luther King Jr. Mural, Overlook Tower   98

East Waco Library Mural   100

Ramad Carter   102

Reverend George Oliver   116

Stevie Walker-Webb   130

Washington Avenue Bridge   141

The editor thanks the following groups for image permissions: the City of Waco for permission to reproduce images of the murals of Martin Luther King Jr. at the Overlook Tower by artist Ira Watkins, the Doris Miller Monument by Eddie Dixon and Stan Carroll, and the kinetic tornado sculpture by artist Mark White; Waco-McLennan County Library for the use of photographs of the East Waco Library mural; McLennan County Courthouse for permission to use photographs of the Courthouse rotunda and mural. Creative Waco provided support for securing permissions. With the exception of the portraits of Reverend Michael D. Babers, Reverend George Oliver, and Stevie Walker-Webb, all photographs in the volume are by Mark Menjívar.

Foreword

Stevie Walker-Webb

I have the great fortune of owning one of my great-great-grandmother's hand-sewn quilts. Some of the patches on the quilt date back to the late 1800s. I discovered the quilt one afternoon while cleaning out my Aunt Ida's basement. Aunt Ida had been using it to protect some of her seasonal home décor—Christmas chalices and gaudy gold table settings that she'd purchased on discount from TJ Maxx.

I remember being instantly drawn to the beautiful, multi-colored tapestry and asking Aunt Ida about its story. She casually shared that it was just a collection of old rags, useful only for protecting her Christmas knickknacks from dust. But there was something about the intentional patterns and the reinforced hem around the edges of the quilt that made me press further. Eventually, Aunt Ida revealed that it was actually her Big Mama's quilt—my great-great-grandmother, Queenie Webb. She told me Big Mama was known for sewing quilts that were as sturdy as tarps, which is why she had used it for years to protect her valuables. I was dumbstruck—it felt like using a hundred-dollar bill to wipe your hands.

I picked the quilt up tenderly and shook off what felt like ten lifetimes of dust. Holding the fabric close to my chest, I inspected the hundreds of patches intricately sewn together. The quilt was heavy, well-made, and beautiful. I could feel my great-great-grandmother's artistry speaking to me across the chasm of time.

This woman, born in the 1880s, whom I have no pictures of but have heard stories about—her grit and tenacity—suddenly felt close. In that moment, as I held her work in my hands, it felt as though she was holding mine. Somehow, through this quilt, she reached across time to affirm her existence within me.

"Big Mama Queen," Aunt Ida said. "Big Mama Queen was always sewing quilts. Back then, Black people had to be resourceful." Aunt Ida told me that these quilts kept them warm during the winter months when they were children, though she joked that they also made her itchy. She now prefers her thousand-thread-count sheets from TJ Maxx over an old, dusty quilt.

When I think about the generations of Webbs who have been warmed, held, wrapped, comforted, nurtured, and protected from the cold under that quilt, it becomes more than just a work of art. "I don't know what happened to all her quilts," Aunt Ida mused. "I think this is the only one left." I tried to convey how special the quilt was, how priceless it was—certainly more valuable than the box of Christmas lights and porcelain dolls it had been protecting. "It's just an old rag," she said. "If you like it that much, you can take it." And so I did.

I took the quilt to a specialty shop, had it steamed, cleaned, and placed in a beautiful wooden frame. It is by far the most valuable thing I own.

Black people live so close to the culture that we are the culture itself, and our nearness to it—our abundant access to it—can sometimes cause us to overlook how important our stories are. Our stories, our songs, our survival, and our culture are our greatest inheritance.

The first time Aunt Ida saw my great-great-grandmother's quilt framed and enshrined on my living room wall, she didn't recognize it. She commented on its beauty and then quickly pieced together that it was the "old collection of rags" she had given me. I joked that she couldn't have it back, and she laughed, saying it didn't match the aesthetic of her home anyway. Still, I could tell she was proud—proud that I valued what the quilt embodies and represents.

What Tyler has done in this collection of interviews about the lynching of Jesse Washington and its historical reverberation within Black Waco is akin to the framing of a quilt. Tyler has taken a story so hideous and dark that it's been relegated to the basement of our collective consciousness and placed it in a new frame. He has taken the misplaced story of Jesse Washington—much like the quilt—which has been used to cover and protect something far less valuable (whiteness) and asked us to revisit it again.

It is no accident that Jesse Washington's name cannot be found in the index of any Texas or American history book. It is no accident that there are no monuments to remember him. His story has been put in the basement to protect the myth of America and shield white Wacoans from the ugly truth that we have all inherited. Through these interviews, Tyler is attempting to reframe the events surrounding Jesse Washington's unjust murder through the lens of Black Wacoans, recovering the story from the basement of our consciousness and placing it in the forefront for all to confront.

My Aunt Ida was too close to the quilt to see its value. To her, it was a pedestrian object, something she grew up with. I think for many Wacoans, the story of Jesse Washington is similarly too close to home to be examined with the rigor it deserves— whether from an anthropological or historical perspective. For some, the story is too painful to look at; for others, too shameful. And for younger generations, its significance may be completely unknown.

Still, for many Wacoans, the name Jesse Washington lives on in legend and folklore. The relationship between his murder and the tornado is often dismissed as an old wives' tale. In short, Jesse Washington is someone we either talk about or avoid altogether, but there isn't enough documented, written history about him.

Perhaps it is Tyler's perspective as an outsider that allows him to look in at a story that many of us Wacoans know—one we grew up with—and approach it with new eyes. As you read the carefully selected interviews, know that you're listening to the unfiltered voices of Black Wacoans across multiple generations. In this book Tyler casts himself not as a storyteller, nor even as an interpreter of what's being said; instead he shows up as a servant archivist. The powerful and wizened voices that make up the collection are the griots; Tyler is the platform on which the speakers are standing so that their voices might be amplified through the rigor of his listening and bearing witness. Thank God he's self-aware enough not to attempt anything beyond that.

As an outsider, there is nothing about Jesse Washington's story that Tyler can take for granted. Which is likely why he has spent more than a decade studying this single story. I hope his dedication to amplifying what happened to Jesse Washington finally writes Jesse into history, once and for all.

Introduction

Tyler B. Davis

A Specter Haunting Texas

The May 1916 lynching of Jesse Washington—the total human catastrophe W. E. B. Du Bois infamously called "the Waco Horror"—marked the nadir of racist violence in Central Texas, as the seventeen-year-old Black teenager and farm laborer was publicly lynched in downtown Waco. Thirty-seven years later, in May of 1953, a tornado paved a pathway of destruction through the city. Upending a local "legend of safety," which held that Waco was protected from natural disaster by the arms of God—the Brazos River—the damage was catastrophic. One hundred fourteen people died and thousands were injured.[1]

Mary Denkins's grandparents may have been the first to notice that the path of the tornado appeared as if it were retracing the path of the Waco Horror.

> 1953. I was in high school. I'll never forget when the tornado hit. My mother was very religious. And her favorite thing [to say] was "when God is working, you must be quiet." The day that they had the news that we were going to have a tornado in Waco, I was at Moore High School, my father came to get me, my sister and I, in an old A Model Ford. He had already picked up my brother and my younger sister. And we got home, my mother made all four of the children get into bed fully dressed, shoes and all. And we all had to

get in the same bed, her bed. And she said, "God is fixin' to work so you all be quiet." We couldn't do anything, no radio, nothing. And I'll never forget, we were home exactly fifteen minutes and the tornado hit, fifteen minutes from the time that my dad picked us up and got home, the tornado hit. And then we heard the roaring and the sirens and the noise and stuff. My dad turned the radio on, and they told how the tornado had destroyed Waco, which it had . . . I can tell you this much. And I don't remember all the details, but I do remember my grandparents and my parents telling me this was the way they lynched Jesse Washington and drug his body around the Square. That was exactly the way the tornado came and ripped up.[2]

Whether or not they were the first to notice, the more striking fact is that Mary Denkins's family was not alone. Many Black Wacoans witnessed the same thing. And with inspiration they insisted this was not a coincidence but an illumination. The devastating tornado became a sign of poetic justice in a place—in *the* place—where racial injustice had been a viciously defining feature. For others, it conveyed prophetic meaning. The whirling tower of wind revisiting the scene of Washington's lynching was a revelation of the justice of God.

> *Everybody who we ask says that same thing. It went the same way.*
>
> —*Michael D. Babers*

Activating Stories from Below

Over the years, traumatic memories of lynching have been held in silence in the Black Waco community, belonging to what Rosemarie Freeney Harding called "the things-too-terrible-to-talk-about." Still, the story of the whirlwind survived, as it was handed on to children and grandchildren. Sometimes retold by elders during especially bad storms or whispered between children during tornado drills at school, deadly weather became associated with the deadlier climate of racism.[3]

The whirlwind story is vintage Texana—what could be more Texas than people struggling with and against God, severe weather, and racism? Add to this the further observation that the story is woven into the fabric of local memory and one might get the impression that it is widely known, perhaps portrayed in public murals or taught in the state social studies curriculum. It is not. In reality, most people, especially white Wacoans, are unfamiliar with the story. Even for those who are familiar with it, the reflex to dismiss it as so much superstition, if not resentment, is ready at hand.

This should come as no surprise, for both the hiddenness of the story and the reflex to dismiss it often express the intentions of the powerful and their warped concept of history. Establishment history is always, in truth, a matter of self-justification. Its interest is in the curation of facts that, when arranged in a certain way, legitimize the actions of those in power and exonerate the legacies of domination they lay claim to. Defenders of establishment history nervously fortify their boasts about the past by hiding or dismissing what cannot be assimilated. The effect is a makeshift repression of truth about people and place in the interest of power: an assurance that lived experiences and stories failing to align with their boasts are denied the dignity of recognition and that resources needed for building a shared future remain unavailable.[4]

Annette Gordon-Reed writes that "there is no escaping the fact that we humans seem to need myths and legends as well as history." *God of the Whirlwind* is concerned with the former—that is, with the need for stories. Rather than focus on diagnosing and unmasking the conceits of establishment history, this book takes a different approach. The contention of *God of the Whirlwind* is that the most powerful and revolutionary challenge to establishment history lies in and through the recovery of alternative stories and histories. "Recovery" here does not mean regaining something lost or forgotten, for the stories tended to have been voiced and they are remembered. Instead, it means receiving stories and histories "from below" with an ear attentive to their full consequence, as they contradict the boasts of the powerful and convey a more expansive world.[5]

When I share that story of Jesse Washington, it's like he's activated. That story is activated. The curiosity in others is activated. It's becoming alive.

—Ramad D. Carter

The whirlwind story has held my attention, as an outsider, for over a decade. I first heard the story one afternoon in North Waco. Having grown up in places without history (history was the stuff that happened elsewhere in most of my social studies textbooks), I wound up living in a city that had too much history, such that it seemed possessed by the hauntings of its past. As we locked the doors after another day working at the youth afterschool program, Stevie Walker-Webb and I talked about the ghosts of Waco, especially the ghosts of the Waco Horror. He then shared the whirlwind story as it had been told to him.

I remember being immediately drawn to it. No doubt my interest stemmed from a fascination with tornadoes, having spent my childhood living through severe storms across the Great Plains. Such fascination, I later discovered, belonged to old family traditions of surveying the skies for prodigies, portents, and providence. But more than an echo of imagination or tradition, hearing the whirlwind story was a consciousness-raising moment. I was struck by the way the story somehow all at once reframed and countered regimes of race by speaking divine judgment upon lynching in the weather. Later, when I found myself back in Central Texas for graduate school, I made this dynamic the focus of my dissertation research. In the context of academic theology, I elaborated the story's significance as an image of a homegrown liberation theology which showed the material risks and possibilities of speaking about God in specific circumstances.[6]

The story now holds my attention differently. In the summer of 2022, I returned to Waco with Mark Menjívar to interview members of the community. The process of speaking with Black Wacoans from different generations about their experiences, memories, and theories shifted my perception of things. I began to see the story in a larger context of community struggles, as just one planet in an expansive galaxy of other stories, historical memories, knowledge, ethical and political commitments, theological convictions, and spiritual practices. Seen in this light, the whirlwind story was part of a deep tradition of building life against and despite oppression. In curating oral history interviews from members of the Black Waco community, *God of the Whirlwind* attempts to appreciate the significance of this tradition as it has been expressed in some of the ordinary and apocalyptic stories Black Wacoans have told about people, God, and, occasionally, the weather.

While I have been affected by one such story, I don't regard my experience as merely subjective. It is better taken, I think, as an effect of the story itself as it prompts a search for new ways of living. Vincent Harding, a historian in the Black freedom movement, insisted that the promise of histories and stories from below is that they may animate the human "search for meaning." Harding understood this search as a rendezvous with the "life-giving forces of the morning" perhaps especially within material, moral, and spiritual despotisms hell-bent on causing suffering, like those of plantation society discussed below. Without it, Harding writes,

> we lose touch with ourselves, our fellow humans, and other creatures, with the earth our mother, and with the cosmos itself. Without the search for meaning, the quest for vision, there can be no authentic movement toward liberation, no true identity or radical integration for an individual people.[7]

The aspiration of this book is less about a potential contribution to what might be thought of as objective or subjective history and more concerned with how community storytelling traditions carry and communicate a kind of knowledge capable of shaping ways of living in the world. This book then asks readers: What is the poetic and prophetic vision expressed by community story-tellers? And if stories are not only about holding the attention of an audience, if they also incite the search for meaning and shape ways of living, what search is being incited and what shape is being recommended?

Ultimately, *God of the Whirlwind* is about the Black Wacoans who have shared their lives and memories. The Black Wacoans contributing to this collection speak for themselves, as members of a community, and from their dynamic experiences. *God of the Whirlwind* recognizes them as "organic intellectuals," as teachers and students of an alternative tradition of social justice theory and praxis. They offer harrowing testimony of surviving plantation sharecropping, Jim Crow injustice, and the terror of lynching; they share the strenuous tragedies, negotiations, and achievements accompanying integration, the persistence of unforgiving systems of economic theft and race, and the life-sustaining power of memories passed on from parents and grandparents; and they communicate a vision for an alternative way of life for the region, one departing from unjust social patterns and untruthful stories that have characterized it for too long. Gathering the voices of Black Wacoans, *God of the Whirlwind* is a book about the community that kept the whirlwind story, and many other stories, as part of the long struggle to imagine and practice a different way of living.[8]

The Dominant Way of Life

Many Black folks, myself included, believe it was God's way of getting justice—not just for Jesse Washington, but for generations of Black people who suffered under racism, segregation, and the legacy of slavery.

—*Stevie Walker-Webb*

Where does the whirlwind story begin? It does not begin in the clouds: the severe storm forming over Central Texas on May 11,

1953. It begins on the ground: the lynching of Jesse Washington in downtown Waco on May 15, 1916. But the roots of the lynching, and so the origin of the whirlwind story, can be traced deeper. "Jesse Washington wasn't the first," Linda Jann Lewis observes, setting the terms for a radical perspective. In this perspective, the destructive patterns that rendered lynching a routine feature of life in this region are understood to be part of the conventions of plantation society. To fully appreciate the whirlwind story and other Black Waco memories and stories that follow, it is critical to recognize the domination of plantation society in Texas, for the memories and stories emerge from and respond to this context.

While plantation society has a relatively recent history in Texas compared to the rest of the US South, it is distinguished by the pace and scope of its expansion in the nineteenth century. In its Texas iteration, the plantation was a system of land monopolization, resource hoarding, and profiteering rooted particularly though not exclusively in the global cotton economy and dependent upon enslaved Black labor, peonage, and exploitation. Its daily violence and routine terror was justified through a dehumanizing racial scheme constructing people as "Black," "white," "Mexican," and so on. Broadly speaking, the accelerated westward movement of the cotton slavery economy before the Civil War, an unstable political identity under New Spain, Mexico, and Texas before eventual annexation by the United States, and an anti-abolitionist political culture combined in the making of Texas as a borderland plantation society.[9]

The heart of the slave economy in lower Southeast Texas stretched into Central Texas. In 1860, enslaved people comprised upwards of 25 percent of the total population in both McLennan and Falls Counties. To the east, Freestone and Limestone Counties were the sites of two of the largest slaveholding plantations in Texas, which were owned by the Stroud family, migrant slavers from Georgia. Logan A. Stroud's plantation in Limestone County held at least one hundred people captive as human property, with Stroud also serving as the agent for another estate with seventy enslaved people. L. M. Stroud's plantation in Freestone County enslaved one hundred and twelve people. One of the last hold-outs of slavery in the defeated Confederate State after the abolitionist victory, this plantation represents a birthplace of Juneteenth. On Monday, June 19, 1865, standing in front of the people he held captive, a weeping Logan Stroud and his daughter read General Order No. 3—the dispatch enforcing the 1863 Emancipation Proclamation—declaring that "all slaves are free." Two contributors to this collection, Linda Jann Lewis and Reverend George Oliver, trace their family ancestry to people who were enslaved on the Stroud plantation.[10]

Just west of Limestone County, McLennan County is home to the city of Waco. Situated where the Blackland Prairies intersect the Brazos River (*el Río de los Brazos de Dios*), Waco fashioned itself as the western frontier capital of the global cotton empire, harnessing abundant resources of the land for the latter's expansion. For much of the last two centuries, the Brazos and Blackland Prairies were fated to the cultivation of the plantation: "lovely rolling prairies, swelling into high mounds, or stretching out in extended ridges of black, rich, sandy loam ready for the [plow] . . . and very productive." The thriving ecology of this patch of earth was received within this society as fuel for the plantation machine. The building of the Texas Cotton Palace, a monument to the agriculture empire and grounds for generations of civic expositions, bears out the city's deep sense of vocation.[11]

> *My grandmother was born in 1863. She really had a slave master. We didn't have a slave master, but we had trouble when I was younger. In the thirties and forties and fifties, Black people in Waco had a hard time in that we were considered second-class citizens, number one. Number two, we were segregated.*
> —*LaRue Dorsey*

The latter half of the nineteenth century witnessed mass migration of white people to Texas, especially from the US South, which outpaced Black migration and ensured demographically the restoration of white planter rule. The radical and systemic commitment to generating wealth through cotton production no matter the human and ecological cost fundamentally shaped life in the region. More than an economy, the plantation aimed to be an encompassing social reality. Daily life was dishearteningly characterized by its conventions: systemic impoverishment, land theft, and resource monopolization; legal and vigilante enforcement of racial segregation; routine racist, gendered, and sexual violence; and a moral and spiritual vision projecting inhuman ways of seeing oneself and others.[12]

In Central Texas, poor and working people have had to survive the brutal features of this way of life. Whites, Mexicans, and Black folks striving to meet basic needs found themselves competing in the confining and ladderless world of plantation capitalism. Black communities in particular have borne the brunt of plantation brutality, first through years of racial slavery and later through the enclosures of postwar plantation society. Merely to achieve subsistence after the white revolt against Reconstruction, Black people working in sharecropping or any other newly created wage labor system would have had to survive all kinds of material hazards—health, storms, pests like the boll weevil, depleted soil, equipment failure, diseases, and drought. Beyond basic material concerns, things did not get easier. Black Wacoans had to survive additionally the everyday practices of violence and punishment endemic to plantation capitalism.[13]

In the aftermath of the Civil War, these practices were manifested most intensely in the horrors of lynching violence. Lynching in Texas in the late nineteenth and early twentieth century must be understood within the history and ambitions of plantation society, which was first honed against Indigenous people and Mexicans before being transformed in the postbellum period as targeted anti-Black violence. Between 1877 and 1950, there were at least 4,084 racial terror lynchings of Black people in twelve Southern states, and more throughout the rest of the United States. Mob violence was not, by any means, only exacted against Black men. Between 1880 and 1930, lynch mobs murdered at least 130 Black women. In Central Texas, 64 Black people were lynched between 1860 and 1929. As with national trends, the 1890s were the peak of anti-Black lynching terrorism in Texas. While mob violence decreased in frequency in subsequent decades, it increasingly took on a public character, as exemplified by the mass of spectators present at the lynching of Jesse Washington.[14]

When my grandfather first moved to Riesel, my grandfather, being a sharecropper, came to town to sell his wares. He always came to the square. On the day that my grandfather came to the square in his wagon, he had one of my uncles with him. He witnessed the beginning of a lynching. He didn't witness the lynching. He witnessed someone dragging a man. I don't know how many times, because I'm sure it's more than once that the dragging occurred because of the nature of the people who lynched at that time. When I say "the nature"—the human nature—we're still trying to become civil. We still have a certain level of civility that we still need to work on, so you're always dealing with that. That day my grandfather left without doing any business. He turned around and left.

—Bettie V. Beard

Stories for an Alternative Way of Life

For over a century, plantation society set the terms for living in Central Texas. Today, while the cotton economy and its stifling debt peonage programs no longer dominate, the broad social patterns it initiated have proven resilient. These patterns have taken various forms in more recent history, including, for instance, the post-integration divestment in Black and poor people's housing, the rise of the prison and punishment industry, and the state's incorporation of extralegal lynching violence in the form of capital punishment.[15]

Nevertheless, the enduring conditions and values set in place by plantation society have not totally defined life. As Linda Jann Lewis reports, Waco has also been a "Black Mecca." Black Wacoans have found ways to oppose plantation society and to live on different terms, especially in and through stories. In community centers and parks, in homes and church buffet lines, in books and convenience store conversations, stories have provided terms not just for making sense of life in the context of vast social suffering but for fostering alternative ways of living.[16]

An account of the many Black Waco stories that have promoted an alternative way of living would include boogie-woogie pianist Sammy Price's childhood remembrance of hearing a mysterious traveling bluesman revise the lyrics to W. C. Handy's lovesick blues song "Hesitating Blues," to sing against the lynching of Jesse Washington. It would include Sutton Griggs's 1899 utopian novel, *Imperium in Imperio*, which astonishingly imagined Waco at the height of lynching violence as the ground zero for a new society for Black people. It would include Lucille Webb telling her grandchildren on stormy nights of a righteous tornado as the hand of God tracing the path of the Waco Horror. It would include the late county commissioner Lester Gibson confronting the cowardice of city and county leaders who refused to remove the lynching image from the McLennan County Courthouse rotunda mural. It would include the long struggle and achievement of grassroots organizations like the Community Race Relations Coalition to tell a truthful public story that acknowledges the history of lynching. It would include the story of Rickey Cummings, a son of Waco currently on death row, writing and envisioning a future where "preventative and restorative measures" define social justice practice in place of the "punitive actions" of the death penalty. To these would be added more stories, some kept close within families and others yet untold. Viewed collectively, this continuous tradition of Black Waco stories voices an alternative social, theological, and spiritual vision for regional transformation.[17]

> *That tornado took that same path down through there. You bet you—I mean, it went straight down Bridge Street. From the river—that bridge that's still standing down there—but it went straight down through there.*
> —*Anthony Fulbright*

> *They said a tornado went through that pathway. The story about Sank—my maternal grandmother, who was his sister, told that to me and two of my cousins when we were maybe about ten years old. I could tell it hurt her to talk about it, but she wanted to tell it.*
> —*Nona Kirkpatrick*

The story Lucille Webb told her children and grandchildren is a significant focus of this collection. This story from below attained power from above, figuring the whirlwind as the hand of God revisiting the very ground of Washington's subjection. The tornado was an illumination of divine justice calling into question the whole white racist plantation way of life that had led to the Waco Horror.

Still, not everyone in Black Waco nor in this collection shares this view of the whirlwind's illumination. The fact that certain memories, stories, and history are shared in this community does not entail harmony or preclude different perspectives. The closer one gets to this story and those who tell it, the more the story proliferates, becoming many stories mirroring many voices. Nona Kirkpatrick's family tradition, for instance, holds to a different version of things. In her family's telling, the tornado retraced the path not of the lynching of Jesse Washington but of Sank Majors—Kirkpatrick's great-uncle—who had been the victim of a racist lynching in Waco in 1905. Others, moreover, hesitate to draw too much meaning from the story. And they do so for different reasons: from an overwhelming sense of the tragedy of the tornado, or out of a view that justice is better achieved through the surer footing of historical reconstruction, so avoiding the potential ambiguities of stories. A feature of this collection is that the story receives multiple theorizations regarding its significance.[18]

> *"Not that people died but that God had something to say about it. God wasn't silent on the story."*
> —*Rev. George Oliver*

John Berger writes that "stories are one way of sharing the belief that justice is imminent." Telling the fearless story of the God of the whirlwind is one way of sharing the belief that the dominant way of life, which has created uninhabitable conditions for so many, is coming to an end. In gathering voices from the Black Waco community, *God of the Whirlwind* aims to recover this and other shared stories from below and, along the way, foster their continued preservation. The more ambitious hope is to grow the recognition that spiritual and material resources needed to address systemic injustices and structured scarcities—resources inspiring searches for meaning as well as social relationships rooted in mutuality, sharing, and love—are abundantly present in stories and traditions from below.[19]

God of the Whirlwind contains eight chapters with nine people from this community; the chapters are adapted from oral history interviews conducted in the summer of 2022. The book is organized by theme into three parts, "Storm," "Story," and "Spirit," with photographs of contemporary Waco taken by Mark Menjívar. "Storm" is composed of chapters by LaRue Dorsey and Linda Jann Lewis who share about the social challenges they have experienced and transformations they have participated in while living in this setting. "Story" relays accounts from Reverend Michael Babers, Bettie Beard, Anthony Fulbright, and Nona Kirkpatrick. Like Dorsey and Lewis, these narrators share their experiences while adding a distinct focus on the tornado storytelling tradition and presenting different views of the story's significance. In the final part, "Spirit," Ramad Carter, Reverend

George Oliver, and Stevie Walker-Webb contribute vantages from a younger generation who inhabit the spirit of the storytelling traditions and offer theorizations of the whirlwind story's meaning. The book's three parts and eight chapters are united thematically by a steadfast commitment to the truth of shared community stories and their enduring power to shape ways of life.

> *Let's just tell the truth about our history. And I think—no, I don't think—I know that the truth will set all of us free.*
>
> *—Linda Jann Lewis*

Part 1
Storm

Chaos in windy grays
through a red prairie.

—Gwendolyn Brooks, "The Last Quatrain
of the Ballad of Emmett Till"

For it is not light that is needed, but fire;
it is not the gentle shower, but thunder.
We need the storm, the whirlwind, and the earthquake.

—Frederick Douglass, "What to the
Slave Is the Fourth of July?"

1

LaRue Dorsey

LaRue Dorsey has dedicated her life to helping young people learn. A giant in Texas education, Dorsey taught for over sixty-two years. For sixteen years, Dorsey directed the renowned LaRue's Learning Center, which supported the education of children from Black and low-income families in Waco. In this chapter, Dorsey recounts her father's vision of education as a vehicle out of poverty, teaching in the era of Jim Crow racial segregation, the challenges and changes that came with integrating Waco schools, and the significance of Black churches and faith in the making of a more just community.

I was born in Waco to Rev. and Mrs. B. F. Gilbert. I graduated from A. J. Moore High School in 1949 and went to Mary Allen College for a BS in '52.[1] I got my master's degree from Texas Southern University in Houston in '58. I taught school for sixty-two years total. In that sixty-two years, I owned a school for myself, called LaRue's Learning Center, for sixteen years. The reason that I started the school is because our kids were having difficulty in public school. I would go out in the hall and see kids sitting out in the hall. I'd say, "Baby, why are you out here?" "Mrs. So-and-So put me out." I'd go ask the teacher, "Could you bring him back in? Because nobody learns anything sitting out in the hall."

I finally decided to start a school, which I kept sixteen years. I had twos, threes, and fours in order to try to get our kids to be ready when they got to public school. I enjoyed every minute of it. During my time having the school, Paul J. Meyer, who was a millionaire here, heard about me. He took a liking to me and what I was doing. In ten years, he helped me with the school by giving a $250,000 grant. I got the interest off that for ten years. At the end of that sixteen years, I closed the school, because people didn't want to pay their bills and I didn't have the money to keep it going. But I enjoyed every minute of the sixteen years.

From the sixteen years, I have kids who were doing everything. They call and tell me what they're doing. From this school, I have three lawyers, four preachers, twenty teachers, truck drivers, barbers, beauticians, opera singers—people doing everything. My thing was for our kids—by the time they got to public school, they would know some of the basics, which was true because my school was nominated to be a top school in the city. Everybody wanted my little children, because they were well prepared. It wasn't me by myself, I had a good staff. When you have good people working with you, you can do something.

My objective was to see that our kids would be considered as top students, and that they could learn. It's not that they couldn't learn, it's just nobody had taken time with our kids. Most of our parents worked two or three jobs trying to make a living, and our kids were on their own. I was a substitute parent because we did everything at my school. We took field trips every month somewhere. I had a curriculum for the four-year-old children—two- and three-year-old children. Everybody took a field trip once a month. The twos went somewhere, the threes went somewhere, and the fours went somewhere, in order for them to see something. Believe it or not, some of our kids had never crossed the Brazos River. I took them across the river, and they thought they'd gone across the Pacific Ocean.

I learned a lot of stuff because I was born poor. We were very poor, but my daddy had a vision for us. The vision was that we got an education. During my time, you had to pick cotton and chop cotton. He told us to get an education, which we did. I'm from a family of five children—I'm the oldest—and all of us have master's degrees or PhDs, except one, and that one did twenty years in the air force. He's very intelligent also. From my brother's children, they all have done very well. Everybody—my brother next to me had two children. His daughter is a CPA. Then my next brother has four children. Two of them are pastors with PhDs, the third boy is a businessman, and the girl is a teacher in Houston. My next brother had three children. One is a principal and one is Kenyatta Gilbert, with a PhD. He teaches in Washington, DC, at Howard University. Then the next boy lives in Houston, employed at Rooms To Go. Then, my next brother had three boys. One owns his own business, one is a parole officer, and the other boy finished San Francisco State University. He works at some kind of store and sells clothes.

Our family has been very blessed in education because of my daddy's dream. My daddy had a vision. My daddy finished high school the year I finished high school, in 1949. He had been in the field and stuff, working all the time as a country preacher who made thirty dollars a week and had a wife and five children. Now, that sounds ridiculous, but that's what it was. When I started teaching in 1952, I took over my daddy's household because my daddy was sick all the time. I ran his house, and I tell people now that back in 1952, when I bought groceries, it took two people to bring the groceries to the car. It wasn't but sixty or seventy dollars. Now, I can bring sixty or seventy dollars' worth out in the car by myself. This is just how times have changed. I had a very happy childhood. After God, family's all you really have. You choose your friends, but God gives you your family. Our grandmother stayed with us. Our grandmother was born in slavery, so she told us a lot of things that would happen to her in slavery. Her time was even worse than what happened to us when I was younger. We've come a long way. Our family has come a long way.

My grandmother was born in 1863. She *really* had a slave master. We didn't have a slave master, but we had trouble when I was younger. In the thirties and forties and fifties, Black people in Waco had a hard time in that we were considered second-class citizens, number one. Number two, we were segregated. We had Black schools, white schools. The white schools got all the stuff, but the Black schools got very little. Yet we had some teachers who were determined that we were going to learn. We were very fortunate in having those teachers back in those days. In that day, it took a whole village to raise children. Our parents knew the teachers, and they gave them permission to do whatever was necessary for us to learn, because we saw these teachers five days a week, we saw them at church on Sunday. They knew us very well, and I appreciate that. During that time, I didn't realize how important it was for us to be educated. But when I got older, I recognized that had we not been, we'd have been in the field the rest of our lives until cotton-picking was over.

Waco was different in that even going to the store to buy clothes, we were not allowed to try the clothes on. You had to hold them up to see if it was going to fit. You couldn't try on shoes, hats, or anything. This was at the average store. It wasn't just one store; this is the way they did. We could not use the restrooms downtown at the stores. You had to go to the interurban railway station. It had an interurban that came through Waco. It was up on Eighth Street. You had to go walk on down First Street where the tornado came through—called Bridge Street. This is where we had to go. You had to walk, like, eight blocks to use the bathroom if you had to use the bathroom. This was typical Waco.

Riding the bus, we had to sit on the back seat. If somebody got on there, we had to stand up and hold the things that you hold onto, because they would have made us get up and let the white people sit down. But this was par for the course during my time, back in the forties and fifties. Until integration came and Mr. Lyndon B. Johnson passed the bill that we could have rights—that's when our people started progressing. They got the chance to have jobs, like your people had jobs. They started making the same money and started buying stuff, because prior to that, you could pick cotton all day for three dollars a hundred pounds. If you didn't pick but a hundred when it first was $1.50 and then it went to three dollars, people thought that they were really rich by that time, you know. They chopped cotton all day long for six or seven dollars a day. That's eight hours. This is what our people were living off of. People said that our people were lazy. They were not lazy. They just didn't have the funds. Most of them had large families back in those days—eight to ten to twelve children. You're trying to feed somebody, trying to buy them school clothes, trying to do different stuff with the little money you had. This was very hard.

We lived out in what they called Butcher Pen back in those days. It's on the other side of La Salle. Our house was the last house before you got to. They had a slaughterhouse where they'd kill hogs and things. At that time, our house was the last house on Gurley Lane, down in South Waco, off of Twelfth Street. This is my home house. This is where we were born—my brother and myself. The other children were born in a hospital, but the two oldest kids were born at home because during that time they had the doctors who came to the house.

I belong to Antioch Missionary Baptist Church, 2814 South Twelfth Street. At that time, it was on Oakwood Street. This is where my membership has been since I was nine years old. I belonged to that church since I was nine. So, I've been through Rev. Richard L. Bailey, Rev. Fabian K. Jacko, Rev. Delvin Atchison, and Rev. J. J. Rector. That's the pastors we've been through. I'll be ninety next month, if the Lord says so. That's how many pastors I've been through. One stayed fifty-seven years. Another stayed, like, fourteen. Thirteen, twelve. We've had a marvelous church because our church was like family. The older people who were in the church, they're all pretty well gone. I'm one of the older people.

They had a lady who'd teach you about the Bible. But she also taught you how to be a girl and what you're supposed to look forward to when you got grown. You had something to do at the church, because the church was the hub of Black culture. You couldn't go anyplace else. You couldn't afford to go anyplace else. The church was the ideal place, because you went to church on Monday. You went to church on Tuesday for choir rehearsal. You went to church on Wednesday for prayer meeting. The people who were on the usher board, they went on Thursday. You had Friday off. Saturday, they would have some play for you to do. You know, some fun baseball games and softball games or something like that. On Sunday, you were back to church. Sometimes, you had three services a day. You had morning service, evening service, and night service, and nobody thought anything about it.

I lived in South Waco, and Moore High School was on where University Drive is now, down on the corner. We had to walk almost three miles to school and three miles back. But we had a gang, walking and talking. At that time, we had to pass by Baylor University. They wouldn't allow us to cross Baylor. They threw rocks at us. So, we had to go around Baylor. This is what it was, even though it was a Christian school, but they still did not like us. The times have changed. I'm glad God let me live to see a change, because it was terrible back in those days. It was just absolutely terrible. When I was a little kid, I went, "Why are they doing us like this?" Because if you cut both of us, we bleed the same red. It's just a color difference. That's what it was. It was color. It wasn't anything to do with our brains or nothing to do with anything. It was just color. But it's better now. It's better.

All on the other side of La Salle Avenue coming down into Gurley, everybody there was Black. It wasn't any white folks and wasn't any Spanish. It was just Black. You knew everybody in that community. Everybody knew everybody, some way or other. You'd walk to school with their children or went to church with them. They had Baptist and Methodist, but we knew all of them. You visited each other's churches. You know, my daddy was a pastor and he would be invited to the Methodist church, because our neighbors were Methodist and they wanted him to come preach. Then they'd come over to our church and we had something special. People just worshiped together. At that time, they showed much love, because something could happen to one, and everybody would show up. If something happened to Mrs. So-and-So and everybody—you'd see all the people coming to see what could they do.

Reverend Bailey licensed my daddy when I was a kid. My dad started pastoring when I was six years old, and his first church was in Clifton, Texas. Shiloh Baptist Church in Clifton, Texas. When he left there, he came to Bremond, Texas, and Chilton, Texas. What they had was, the second and fourth Sunday, he was in Chilton. The first and third Sunday, he was in Bremond. He did that forty-some years, until he died. He pastored those two churches.

My stepdaddy left town because of Jesse Washington. They hanged him up on the courthouse yard, downtown. He thought they was going to hang him next. He was, like, sixteen at that time. He was afraid. All Black people were afraid that anything—because you couldn't prove what actually happened. They wouldn't take your word, what I'm saying, and most people didn't have a lawyer. They couldn't afford a lawyer. Plus, lawyers wouldn't take them, anyway. Jesse Washington—that was before my time, but everybody talked about—my grandmother and those who were living. My dad and others, they went down—well, they stayed downtown and saw it. They all flew home, because they didn't know who the next one he was going to grab to hang. They said that he had whistled and had done something to the white lady, and they hanged him. So that was, you know, scary. It has been scary, particularly for Black men, and it's still scary for Black men.

One of the things that I like to do is for culture to learn culture. You know, come to my house and visit me, and I come to your house. You know me. We get to know each other. I have some white friends that I have done it with and stuff like that. But there are some people, my race and my age, who would not dare to go to white folks' house. They're scared to death because they were raised differently. Well, I was raised—because by me teaching, I met white people. Because of me being on the city council, I met white people. Because of having a school, I met white people. I've met white people all kind of ways.

After the Civil Rights Movement, I saw people doing better and having more. You were treated the same way, because prior to that time, you couldn't go to a restaurant to get anything to eat. You knew you had to go behind the barn or somewhere. You'd go in a back alley, and they'd hand you something out through the window. It was the same way. It wasn't any different, as far as I was concerned, particularly about eating stuff and particularly about using the bathrooms. You could be driving down the highway going somewhere. You pull in the filling station, and they wouldn't let you use the bathroom. We did that one time. My daddy put the gas nozzle in the gas tank. The man said, "Can't use the bathroom," so Daddy took it out. He had about ten cents worth of gas in it. He drove across the street. The man across the street said, "That's the way I make my money. He won't let you all use the bathroom, but I don't care what color you are. You can use the bathroom." So, we got the gas. Then we learned, going to stop at his filling station, because there were places who wouldn't let you. They wouldn't let you even get any water and stuff like that.

Integration was strange in the way Waco did it. They took different ones of us from Black schools and put us in white schools and put the white person in our school. This was after Christmas, which was bad. They should have waited till the end of the year, because the little kids weren't used to a Black teacher, and our kids weren't used to a white teacher. We had a lot of problems with that. The little kids didn't know how to accept me. One little boy drew back to slap me—I never had a child try to slap me—because I wouldn't let him see his grades. I had to tell him, "Son, you don't want to go there. You don't want to do that." We had a lot of—because they went, "What's your name?" At that time, I was Mrs. Walker. "Well, what's your other name?" I said, "That's what my name is: Mrs. Walker." They wanted to call me by my first name, because that's what they called their maids: by their first name. "You can call me that or just say 'ma'am' or whatever, but you're not calling me by my first name." We had trouble. We had a hard time from January till school was out. The white teachers had a hard time, because the Black kids didn't know them either. To me, that was the wrong thing to do. They didn't ask us. They just told us to do it.

I came to South Waco Elementary School, from that school. Even the principals were different. Now, one of the principals was very nice. He was a white fellow. He was very nice, but the other person, he had problems with Black people because I think he thought we didn't know what we were doing. I told him one day, "Sir, we taught school here in the same city. We're doing the same thing that you do in school." But he couldn't get that, because he was just used to us being maids and cooks and stuff. He wasn't used to a Black person being an educator.

They pulled all of us who had master's degrees and higher degrees and sent us to their school, and we got their teachers who had just started and sent them to our school, which was wrong. That made our kids get further and further behind, because we had all these people with more than twenty years of experience who had to leave to teach at the white schools, and those young teachers sent to the Black schools had like two or three years. I'm not saying the teachers were bad; they just didn't have any experience. They sent all of us who had a master's to the white school—and had many years of experience. I had more than twenty-some-odd years in. They sent us all over there and then sent their kids who were just in their first or second year out of college. Those young teachers hadn't ever been with Black people. They didn't know what the kids were doing, and the kids were acting ugly. Some of them would act ugly. But for real, some of their kids was acting ugly, too. But they don't tell that part. They just tell the part about Black folks acting ugly.

Our kids had had no experiences. The kids that I was teaching, they'd come and say they had been to Colorado on the weekend to go skiing. Well, our kids didn't know about skiing. You know what I'm saying? They'd never even seen it except on TV. They've never been. Those kids had so much advantage. They had seen so much and had done so much. That's the reason, when I had my school, I did all kind of things with those kids, to show them how people live. I even took my kids out to dinner, little four-year-old children. The little boys had to pull the seat out for the little girls and stuff. I was teaching them manners, where you go out and how you act when you're out. I even took them on an Amtrak train trip to Fort Worth to see the sunken garden there and brought them back. Just stuff like that. We went to the airport, to let them see an airplane landing. During that time, the pilot let us get up on the plane with the children. Stuff like that, the kids never will forget. They hadn't seen stuff like that.

See, everything I made a teaching lesson, because our kids didn't know—hadn't seen anything. I took them to Safeway store for shopping, because the kids had never been in Safeway. They'd go to the store, but they stayed in the car. The folks wouldn't let them in that store. So, I took them in there to see, and they were just amazed. We studied about a pineapple, and then we went in there and found out how many different ways could you find a pineapple in the store. Then we bought a pineapple, came back, and ate the pineapple. These were teaching experiences for my kids.

When we integrated, I had a lot of Spanish-speaking kids too. They were the same as our kids: behind. They couldn't speak English. I took my Crock-Pot to school and cooked a meal, because we talked about the story where the man came to town, he wanted some food, and they didn't have any food. So, he got a big pot and set it down and put a brick off in there—a rock—stone soup, as he called it—put the stone off in there. And he said, "I sure wish I had something to go in there." A lady said, "Well, I got some onions." Somebody said, "I got some of this." When he got through, he had a whole pot of soup. This was showing how people cooperate, and I showed them how you cooperate. We got to actually eat our soup that day.

See, I love teaching. You can tell that I love teaching, because I like to see little kids blossom. They look at you strange because they don't understand what you're saying. When they get it, it's just like little flowers. They just open up.

Some got arrested, but they sat there during the time when Martin Luther King and his group were doing that. Some of the people in Waco—some Black people in Waco were doing that.

They wanted to get some of the rights that they didn't have, so they sat in. And then my brother was involved with getting the schools integrated. Robert—the one that finished Baylor—first Black graduate—he was involved with suing Waco ISD to get Waco where the kids could go to school together. John Winfield Walker from Arkansas was the lawyer for that group. He got it where they—a lot of people didn't like it and Robert was threatened with his life. They set his house on fire. He was a cripple in the bed, and some people got him out the bed when they saw the house on fire. But he got a letter from the Ku Klux Klan and all this stuff, because some people didn't want change.

Most people are afraid of change because they don't understand change. There is a way that seems right to man, but it's not. You have to follow the rules. Well, the rules they had set up, we had to follow the rules. But some of the rules were so different. You can do this, but I can't do this. But it's the same rule. That's the way it was. They had trouble with this—even naming the school because Blacks wanted to keep A. J. Moore, and they turned it to Jefferson-Moore. A. J. Moore was named after a Black principal. When it integrated, they changed that from—they kept Waco High, but they changed our school to Jefferson-Moore. The people had a problem with that.

The night that they had the tornado, we didn't have TVs and stuff then. We had a radio and we heard it scratching. I kept trying to change stations. It was scratching. I said, "What in the world is this?" Finally, they said, "The tornado that hit Waco—" I said, "Oh, God." That was, like, at eight o'clock at night, and I stayed up all night trying to get my family on the phone. I didn't get them until four o'clock that morning, and my daddy said all of them were well, okay. But when I came back, the whole downtown path was knocked out. Stuff was knocked down. It was strange because the whole—going through Elm Street like that, down—it was called Bridge Street—all the Black businesses—all that stuff was torn up and it was gone. Like, the furniture store, R. T. Dennis and Co., Inc., all that was right down that path going down toward the river. All that was gone, and they never built those places back.

We used to vote in Mecca Drug Store. That's where Negroes voted. During the time they first started voting, they charged $1.75. You had to pay to vote. Then it went down to seventy-five cents and then finally got to be free. I don't know whether your people were paying, but we had to pay to vote. People were standing out in the hot sun to get a chance to have the privilege of voting, because they hadn't been able to vote before.

I really hadn't heard the story about the tornado following the path of the lynching. I heard that the Huaco Indian had said they never would have any tornado because of the way the city was built, but it was one of the biggest tornadoes they ever had in history—because it really did happen. People here that saw it and lived through it—Waco has been through a lot of stuff, a lot of different things that have happened, that people been through, but it has endured. Many went through a lot of strange things that they had, so you had to learn how to live by faith. You walk by faith and not by sight. You know, you walk by faith. You got to believe if he said it, he's going to do it. He's going to—if he say he's going to take care of you, he's going to do that. Older Black people had faith in God. That's the only place we had to go, really, the church, and the pastors then told you what the word of God said. He said that we were all equal in his sight and we had to wait on him. He answers "yes," "no," and "wait." You just have to wait and see what he's going to do. If he promised he's going to do something, he does it, but he does it on his own time, not according to our schedule but on his schedule.

When I was growing up, women wore hats and things like that, because that's the only place they had to dress up to go. You didn't have anyplace else to go. You didn't have clubs like they have now, like nightclubs and places like that. Well, the ones they had were called joints. The men went but the ladies didn't go. Black people dressed up to go to church. So, you say—ask me, "Why y'all wear hats all the time?" It's because that was the only place we had to go to wear a hat. You wanted to look your best because—my daddy always said, "When you go to God's house, look the best you can."

You don't want to be disrespectful with what you're wearing. You want to look like he's somebody, because he is somebody.

Some of the sororities, fraternities give scholarships and things for kids. That has sustained Waco culture. Then the library has been good, because kids can go over there when they can't go anyplace else. They have a nice place for them, since they have computers and things now. During that time, you had a place to read, and the kids got so much for reading so many books. That sustained our kids. The kids got a chance to bowl and skate. That gave them some friendship, and that sustained our culture in Waco.

One of the things about most Black people in Waco: when they finish high school and college, they don't come back to Waco. They go somewhere else. That's the reason Waco's culture is pretty well older. Our young people go somewhere else where they can get more money and they have more things to do, because they say Waco's too quiet. This is one of the things. This is what has sustained Waco: kids going to movies and bowling. At my church, what I did, the kids who had done well, I asked the pastor, "Will you take them skating? Take them bowling or something, so the kids know that you have some fun at church too." They started—you had to maintain a certain grade and come to so many meetings at the church, and then you'd get a chance to go. All the kids were loving it. You know, they loved it. They'd get a chance to be one of the ones that'd go skating or bowling or to the movies. This is something that has sustained the kids. The kids did well in football and baseball and basketball, so people got a chance to go and see their children do well. This has sustained Black culture too.

I think God's been very kind to Waco. Even through the tornado, he has preserved Waco, because all the tornadoes and all the storms and stuff that has happened to other places, he could have torn Waco up more, like he's tearing up other places. He has really sustained Waco. He's been very kind to Waco.

We have the opportunity to be on some of the committees and boards and things now, which wouldn't have happened back in the sixties and stuff. I was on the city council board, and then I've been on a lot of other community boards and stuff like that, working with people of all descriptions, all colors, and everything. It's better. I was selected by my community for this, because I certainly didn't volunteer. I was selected.

It still has a long ways to go, because some of the things are reverting from what it was. It's going backwards, because there are some people who now are going backwards in the progress we've made. But, you know, all—I see that, too. But mostly, it's better than what it was in the sixties and seventies. Well, I think okay, except one thing: we don't do enough for the homeless. This is my prayer: that they would give a building for the homeless people out here in the 105-degree weather standing out in the sun, that they have a place to go cool. It's enough buildings in Waco vacant that they can put in a cooling system. The city could do more, at least open up one place for all these women, men, and children standing out here in this hot sun. That's my personal thing that I think they could do, but they don't ask people like me. They probably wouldn't hear me anyway. Because when I was on city council, we tried to get a place for the homeless. They never did do it. We really need a place for them.

Now, they have My Brother's Keeper Homeless Shelter. Well, they don't have many people coming in there now to stay, since they have that COVID. But it's just so many people can stay there, and that's it. They have to leave at six o'clock in the morning and can't come back till six o'clock that evening. You see what I'm saying? We need someplace, because you don't ever know what's going to happen to you. See, all of us are just one paycheck away from being homeless. You could lose your home through fire, through anything, and you're out on the streets. Like me, I don't have any children, nothing like that, so unless my nieces or somebody would come, I'd be homeless. My husband's dead, so I would be out on the street. So, I'm saying, be careful how you treat these folks, because it could be you. I always put myself walking in folks' shoes. How do I want to be treated? I want to treat you the same way.

Until we have compassion—you may not like the folk. That's not the problem. It's what are you doing for service for people. You know, God hadn't asked us to like folk. He said love them.

2

Linda Jann Lewis

A descendant of people who were enslaved on the Stroud Plantation, a participant in the revolutionary freedom movements of the 1960s, and a self-described Catholic hippie thriving in "the Vatican City of Baptists," Linda Jann Lewis reflects on what she calls the richness, hilarity, and tragedy of the Black Waco community. Lewis's expansive political knowledge is grounded in decades of grassroots activism. Lewis insists that in the face of persistent social injustice, we must return to the question of action: "What are we going to do about it?"

I am a fifth-generation Texan.[1] I am a descendant of the Stroud plantation, which was huge.[2] My paternal line of the family—my grandmother and grandfather Harrison and Rebecca Giddings-Lewis—moved to Waco during World War II. Their only son, Odell Lewis, went into the army. Like a lot of Black GIs still do today, he sent money home. They moved from "the country"—Calvert, Texas—into Waco, into what we call Old East Waco—an original part of East Waco. In 1945, while my dad was in the army, the Lewises moved here, on Houston Street.

I'm the oldest grandchild of six siblings and an additional sister. My upbringing in Waco, Texas was in a totally segregated, protected environment. My life revolved around church, school, home, and, as I grew up, social clubs—because that was our life. I'm still at this property today. It is across the street from the

37

State Tabernacle of the Church of God in Christ, the COGICs. The building that housed the school for the colored—prior to the tornado—survived the tornado. I can see it out of my living room window right now. We were not a part of Waco Independent School District gerrymandered lines. Faulkner Lane that intersects my street and my block was the La Vega Independent School District. From first grade until I graduated in 1965, I had an excellent education in segregated schools in Waco, Texas, that were part of the La Vega School District because of segregation. Most of our teachers had master's degrees and PhDs. We are the children of that.

I attended George Washington Carver High School. It was the pride of the La Vega School District. It only lasted thirteen years, but in those thirteen years, we had a nationally award-winning high school band. We won state baseball championships—state football, something. The graduates of that school have gone on to do marvelous things. I was the 1965 valedictorian. The salutatorian, Charles Perkins, and I went to the University of Texas—entered the University of Texas at Austin in the fall of 1965 on scholarships. Charles Perkins was one of the first two African Americans in the famed UT Longhorn Band. I got free tuition, because, first of all, I was a valedictorian of the high school. Secondly, because my name was Linda Lewis. In the sixties, they couldn't distinguish that that was a Black person. It's sort of like Heman Marion Sweatt. That was the beginning of my education.

My education was in those totally Black schools that were part of the La Vega School District. Finally, twenty years later—twenty years after *Brown v. Board of Education*—La Vega School District made a trade or some kind of contract with Waco ISD. Waco ISD closed down G. W. Carver, the plant, [and] the school buildings. It reopened as a community center for a period of time. And then finally, [laughs] because it was a school building—finally, in some later years, I want to say—I wasn't living here, but maybe thirty years or so, G. W. Carver was reopened as a middle school.

We lived in a very isolated community. I now look at it as growing up in Soweto, South Africa. It was a completely contained, segregated community, but it was a Black township. We had our grocery stores. We had doctors, dentists, newspapers, and a church on every other corner. My dad belonged to the Masonic Lodge Number 92. There were sororities and fraternities. I'm a beneficiary of the early schoolteachers and professional women who were AKA, members of Alpha Kappa Alpha sorority.

We—children walk this neighborhood, but as a young girl, I was not allowed to walk the streets in my community by myself. I had to be with other children my age. It was better if there were boys in the group. That was just to protect us, because my grandfather—who was from Montgomery, Alabama and a World War I veteran, and had seen a lot more—had the attitude that Black men need to do whatever was necessary to prevent their wives and daughters from having to cross the river and work for white people. Because once they crossed the river, there was no more protection. If anything happened to the Black females, it was your word against a white man's. You were going to lose. So, I was aware of a lot of limitations in terms of where I could go, who I could go with. Until I was sixteen, I could not cross the Brazos River unless I was with an adult.

The other thing about growing up in this kind of community is you see all kinds of Blackness in its richness. You see all kinds of Blackness in its hilarity. You see all kinds of Blackness in its tragedy. And so, you know, from the community leaders to the neighborhood wino. Richard Pryor's right. We had a neighborhood wino. You see all kinds of people and they look like you. There were so many descendants of the Stroud Plantation that came to town. A lot of the people were related to us. There's a joke about—white people have relatives and Black people have cousins. Your grandparents and your great-grandparents will say, "That's your cousin." It's only now with DNA—AncestryDNA—that we're finding out how we are cousins. What that meant was that within every two or three blocks, there was someone who looked like you who was either related to you, attended your church, family provided services, or married somebody in your family.

I grew up in Greater Mount Olive Baptist Church. My mother had a first cousin who was an incredible singer—gospel singer.

She and a trio, they modeled themselves after the Clara Ward singers. They actually produced some gospel records, because Word Records was here. One city block—so, the church music—I call Waco the Vatican City of Baptists. Although, growing up across the street from the Church of God in Christ—in the summer, they had their state convocations. Back in the olden days, we called them "holiness." Their services went on till one, two a.m. They had musical instruments. The COGICs are some of the most renowned gospel singers up until today. We could sit in our front porch on our yard until we went to sleep to listen to that.

One city block from—east of the Church of God in Christ—was our Chitlin' Circuit Club called Walker's Auditorium. The Walkers attended our church, Greater Mount Olive. Their only child was a girlfriend—classmate and friend of my cousin. So, a lot of singers came through Waco. Ike and Tina Turner were here a lot. Bobby Blue Bland and B. B. King—because it was the Chitlin' Circuit. Mr. Walker—Herbert Walker—who owned the establishment, expanded and put out a patio with loudspeakers. But he went up on the price, I believe, from two dollars to two dollars and fifty cents. People said, "That's too much money to see Ike and Tina Turner, B. B. King, and somebody else."

So, our house is perfectly situated in the center of where Walker's Auditorium is. People would come, bring their chairs, sit in our yard, and listen to—because the singers and the Chitlin' Circuit musicians, you could hear them from the loudspeakers on the patio. From the R&B greats, to gospel singers, to Dr. Keith Elkins, PhD in music—was our music director at Carver High. Our choir was outstanding. He taught us Latin, *Adoramus Te*. He taught—between our band director and our music director, we learned how to read music. Because Paul Quinn College was there, A. J. Moore High—the oldest and larger Black high school—had the Harry T. Burleigh chorus. They did concerts at Paul Quinn College. People came from out of town to Paul Quinn College. There was rich music everywhere.

Not only was there music, but the Negro Baseball League played in Waco on Negro Day at the Katy Ballpark that's now across the street from the famous Magnolia Silos. But the Negro Baseball League—and then, besides Walker's Auditorium, there were little Black cafes and what they call honky-tonks—because during my childhood, there was James Connally Air Force Base. There were the early Black airmen and the Black folk that worked on planes. They came from all over the country to James Connally. Fort Hood is only thirty miles away. Black soldiers came to town. There is a place in East Waco off of Highway Six that I'm told that Nat King Cole came to but that Black people were not allowed to go there during the early fifties and sixties. But somebody's father worked there and said he actually—and, of course, we all know that when Joe Louis was in the army he frequented Waco. Of course, Doris Miller in the navy. Before he was killed, he was on a tour with the NAACP and raising money and bonds. When he was in town, there was a lot of activity.

So Waco was a Black Mecca. You know, as Maya Angelou says, it's a whole lot of fun being Black on a Saturday night in Waco. It is about three miles—Waco has been dry up until—I was working at the legislature in Waco when you could finally buy alcohol in Waco. But it's three miles from the line between the City of Waco and Lacy Lakeview—the line where all the liquor stores existed. I was long-term friends with Governor Ann Richards, who, when she went to alcohol rehab, said, "Well, I grew up in Lacy Lakeview. What did—why didn't you expect me to become an alcoholic?" You could buy alcohol there. All you had to do was cross what is now Lake Shore Drive.

The editor of the *Waco Messenger*—I was a Sunday school secretary—told me that he would pay me and one of my friends to hand out flyers—again, two Black girls walking the streets in East Waco. I needed to have somebody with me. That was just the unspoken rule. So, I got my best friend. He paid us twenty-five cents per street—not twenty-five cents per block but twenty-five cents per street. We walked East Waco streets and put out what we now call door hangers—flyers—about people going to vote for Lyndon Johnson. We did not go to the projects, because if you didn't own property, you couldn't pay poll taxes and you couldn't vote. I don't remember how much money we made, but can you imagine being in maybe the sixth grade and making money because of politics?

My mother's sister, Aunt Roberta, lived in Austin, Texas, and she was a schoolteacher. *Sweatt v. Painter*—Heman Marion Sweatt—was decided in 1950. It is the template for *Brown v. Board of Education* in 1954. Roberta taught at the elementary school across the street from Huston-Tillotson—now Huston-Tillotson University. Her best friend was a woman from Waco, Bertha [Sadler] Means. She was Miss NAACP. In 1950, when *Sweatt v. Painter* was decided, the Black professionals in Austin that already had undergraduate degrees went to UT in the graduate school. That was the first—the law school and the graduate schools were the first schools that were open.

Then, in 1956, the first undergraduate class at the University of Texas was opened. I knew the story of *Sweatt v. Painter*. I knew that Thurgood Marshall and the NAACP were the reason for that. My high school chemistry teacher, Jafus Pitt Cavil Sr., had been a captain in the army. He used his GI Bill to go to UT and get his master's in chemistry. I tell the story that when we were in the seventh grade, Jafus Cavil started brainwashing me and the salutatorian that we could go to UT and succeed. And not only that, it was our duty to be an honor to the race and show those white folks we were just as smart as they were. Mind you, 1965 was when Black was beautiful. Nineteen sixty-five is when corporate America was going to Black campuses recruiting folk. Nineteen sixty-five was when the revolution was going on. People were going to Africa.

There we were, less than two hundred freshmen—two hundred all together in twenty-eight thousand white students at the University of Texas. But we knew what our legacy was. So, I became very active in the UT NAACP, UT Young Democrats, and I placed in Alpha Kappa Alpha. I'm still involved in those three organizations, because my life has taught me that progress is incremental. You get gains and you get setbacks, but you don't stop. You can't go backwards.

I remember our church raising money to contribute to the Southern Christian Leadership Conference. There were some incidents in Waco where we raised money for a Black boy that was accused of raping a white woman when I was in middle school or high school. Once I got to Austin and to UT—and because we read a lot, you know, we had three television stations and radio and we read a lot—I was always amazed about decolonization and what was going on in African countries. I started taking a worldview—and to join Alpha Kappa Alpha—and to know the history. There were chapters forming in Africa—all over the world. The first international AKA chapter was in Liberia. Having access to the university of the first class and having access to their research and their information widened my worldview.

I also understood—began to understand—the economics of cohorts and class. Growing up in East Waco, class was not that much of an issue. We were Black. My awakening to class divisions came during my education at the University of Texas. My parents would call—my aunt lived there, uncle, cousin. I had family in Austin, but I lived in the dorm the first year. My roommate from Waco and I were in an apartment the second year. We were the first Blacks to live in those apartments. I just tell people, if you were in my generation and you went to a predominantly white institution, you were the first Black to do something. So that was just—we just accepted that, you know? We didn't take "no." "Why can't you rent to us?" I think I talk about that in *No Apologies* but here is my first reality check on class.[3]

My parents would call me once a month. That was a luxury, because it was a long-distance call. But they wanted to know, how was I doing? How were the white people treating me at UT? I loved my sociology class. I ended up majoring in—double-majoring in sociology and early childhood. So, here's my conversation with my mother. I said, "Well, classes are going fine," and, you know, talk about my classes, "but I'm just going to go"—this is the early part of the semester—"I'm just going to have to go and drop this sociology class." I liked the class, but the professor was talking about classes—lower class, upper class, middle class, and the poor. "Mother, he said we were poor. We—based on what he said, we are poor! We're not poor!" My mother said, "You are poor. You just didn't know it. You need to go back to that class and find out what you can do about being poor." I had no concept until I was a freshman at UT that I was poor, because my dad had two jobs.

My father used to put us in the car and drive us around. As I said—we had a neighborhood wino. Sunday after church or something, he would drive us around and the drunks would be waking up or be on the streets or whatever. Or he would drive us to areas in town where the houses were really run-down and there was a lot of poverty. His attitude to us—his children—was that you can always be nobody or you can always do nothing. But that's not why I sacrifice—why your grandparents sacrifice. You have to do better. My grandparents always said to me—I lived next door to them—that it was my job to succeed. To do better than their generation and my parents' generation.

So, the prevailing attitude was, I'm going to help you get the best education that you can. I want you to take that education, get out of Waco, and don't come back. Make your mark somewhere else, because it's not fair here. It's going to take a long time for it to be equal. It took them over twenty years after the laws said we need—with all deliberate speed—to integrate our schools. So, go to college. Make friends. Make alliances with people who are doing what you think you want to do as a career. Go make your mark.

For me, there was already proof of that. My father and Congresswoman Eddie Bernice Johnson's father worked together at the Veterans Hospital. She went to nursing school, but she couldn't work at the VA because her father worked there. She went to Dallas Veterans Administration Hospital. She was the first Black nurse—chief psychiatric nurse—at the major hospital there. From there, she went to the legislature. She was one of the eight elected in 1973. So, that was proof of that. We looked up to the kids older than us that left Waco and did good. My life has taught me that there's no such thing as never, because I was one of those people that was never coming back to Waco.

So, there were class differences, and I was a little Black princess. Not only did I have my parents, but schoolteachers. The members of AKA when we were in high school did a marvelous thing. One of the symbols of our sorority is twenty pearls. In the summer we were in the tenth grade, they took ten girls from Moore High and ten girls from Carver High. They started preparing us for college. They taught us all the things that I imagine white girls learn in Junior League or whatever. They taught us how to walk, how to talk, how to be in integrated company. The first live performance I saw was because the AKA Twenty Pearl Project took us to the Waco Civic Theatre. I'd seen things at Paul Quinn—the first live integrated performers. They began exposing us to the world to come.

I always say that the teachers and the neighborhood leaders would say to us, "We want you to be prepared for when the integration comes," like it was coming on a train or bus or an airplane. You're not going to live in the world that we lived in. You're going to have to compete with, work with, mix and mingle with people of other races. I think for me—and I think for some of my peers—we were prepared psychologically. We understood that there was nobody better than us. That was always the lesson. That was always the message. There's nobody better than you.

Angela Davis and Nina Simone were the two Black women that I so identified with. It's ironic. My mother was a Black beautician, so straight hair would make you more acceptable to the white people. My hair's been any way that a Black female's hair can be. It's of a very thick and curly texture. I didn't like any of that. When I went to UT, the freshman girls all had to take swimming. I didn't have a car. There was no Black beautician on campus. It was just—my mother thought she had failed in life because I had an afro. I had an afro out of necessity. I was in the swimming pool twice a week. And Angela Davis had this afro. She was so intelligent. She was an intellectual. Then Nina Simone was just so outrageous in her "African-ness." Visually, those were the two women I related to. Of course, I listened to all of the things and read her books.

My degree is actually from the same university as President Lyndon Johnson's, Southwest Texas State, today Texas State University. Some of my professors had been in LBJ's cabinet. The woman who was my counselor in early childhood education designed Head Start. I was the teaching assistant for the head of the philosophy department, Dr. Keith Lovin, who went to undergraduate at Baylor and got his PhD at Yale. I started off as a student worker aide. Then, my senior year—because I was older and had transferred a bunch of hours—I was actually his teaching assistant. I graded papers for him. I graded papers for him in philosophy of religion. He had some serious surgery and he hired me as his teaching assistant. He told me, just based on my perspective in the papers I wrote about religion—because at that point, the world had opened up. I was trying to reconcile all of the Baptist brainwashing I had with doctrines. So, I read everything. I read all of Immanuel Kant. I read all of the theology and philosophy issues. I had lots of questions. As it progressed—and he knew about my "militancy" and Angela Davis—he got me to apply to Yale. I was a candidate—a finalist for a fellowship to Yale for philosophy. That was the summer of 1974. I was the office manager for Wilhelmina Delco, the first African American elected to the Texas House of Representatives. Ann Richards came over and showed us how to run a campaign, because we really didn't know what we were doing—but I had an automobile accident two weeks before the May primary and was out of commission for a period of time. I could not go and defend or compete—to Yale. I think it was a Danforth Foundation fellowship. I guess God knew exactly where he wanted me to be placed, because that's the summer I cussed out the most powerful politician in Texas—Bob Bullock. Turned my career in another direction.

Religion has historically been a function of power and money. In my view, we wrap it up in a nice present and say, "This is what God wants." I describe myself as a hippie Catholic. I did convert years ago, but I'm more concerned now at this phase in my life with what people do rather than what religion—what religious flag they hold up. I really do. I say that my religion is whatever makes you a better person and takes you away from being violent and angry and evil. Remember, preachers in the Black community—the men who drove nice cars, had nice clothes—were the preachers and the pimps. The other men had jobs, hustles, whatever. And musicians and entertainers—they were the more free. They were the more—they were the power brokers.

Living on this property in the original house, some things happened to us that are, to this day, not explained. That white building across the street, the original house that I lived in here, and my grandparents' house were the only structures standing after the tornado. Everything from around us was flat. They say that we were in the eye of the tornado. We still had walls and damage, but everything else was flat. Just in this little circle here. What I heard about Jesse Washington from the older people and the church people was that they drug him from Robinson through Baylor campus—and that Baylor is cursed. There were Black people—some of them in my circle, relatives, grandparents—that just discouraged going on the Baylor campus, because the spirits were still there.

There are stories also that they hung Black—Jesse Washington wasn't the first; he was just the last—they hung Black folk from that famed suspension bridge. When I returned to Waco in 1991 after having not really lived here since 1965, I was appalled to see that the city of Waco had that suspension bridge as their emblem. It was the logo for city staff. I was senior city staff. My boss was always giving me one to wear at city meetings. I would bring them home and put them in the jewelry box, because I didn't want to glorify that suspension bridge. Just a difference in the perspective of an older Black person versus an older white person. I remember that Lyndon Olson said Oscar Du Conge—who was the first Black on the city council and was voted by the city back in the days when the city council voted for—chose the mayor—rather than the people—that Oscar Du Conge said to him, "Lyndon, we Black people don't have the fondness for that suspension bridge that you white people do." He told him the story of Blacks hanging from that bridge.

I knew about Jesse Washington. I knew because of my NAACP education and Ms. Bertha Means about Elisabeth Freeman, an NAACP field organizer who was a white woman. When they sent out telegraphs saying that the lynching was going on, she drove from Dallas to Waco to investigate. Because she was a white woman, they assumed she was on the side of the lynchings. That's how—of course, you know folk made postcards and photographs of the lynching and sold them—but that's how the story of Jesse Washington made national news. It was through an NAACP field organizer. So, we've always had white advocacy. The NAACP was founded by lawyers, abolitionists, and, in today's parlance, "I want to be a good anti-racist" allies. The legacy of people working together to stop and to avenge racist murders and brutality is still alive today.

We were proud revolutionaries, because "revolution" means radical change. So, we failed miserably at radical change. But there's still the need for change. I know that it is my job to pass on what I've learned based on my experiences to the next couple of generations. Because millennials are the largest cohort since baby boomers—there are 75.4 million millennials. Between six and eight million of them live in Texas. It's the number one place where millennials are moving to. It is so true that if you don't know your past, you're going to repeat it. I'm having these kinds of conversations with my millennial friends. I'm blessed to work with the Baylor NAACP. I have interns. I'm blessed to be involved with the undergraduates—Alpha Kappa Alpha members and Divine Nine members. So, these are the conversations I'm having. Yes, George Floyd was your generation's Emmett Till—is your generation's Emmett Till.

As we said in the sixties, we would spend two hours in the Black room at the University of Texas talking about the evils of "the man" and the evils of what was going on. The question was, "Okay. We've spent two hours intellectualizing on this. What are we going to do about it?" The mantra that we developed in the sixties certainly applies today: we must move from anger to action.

Demographics and time are on our side. In my professional career, I went to a national conference in the 1980s. The national census demographer told us that by 2020, white people will no longer be the majority in this country—the people who, you know, Caucasian white people. That has come to pass. It certainly has come to pass in Texas.

Not only has that come to pass, but we must revisit the story of America. I am ever blessed and grateful to have lived this long. I plan to live longer so that we can start looking at the issue of race. It was an invention by the colonizers. Before global colonization, people were identified by their country or community of origin. The story of America is not about white people. The story of America is about Indigenous people, who've been here for forever. The story of America is about all of the children of the plantation and slave masters, starting with George Washington. We Black people always laugh, because we know somebody—or we've heard the stories of the people—who were the products of this wonderful name that they call it, miscegenation. It was actually rape of some African woman or some Mexican woman who looked Caucasian enough to pass for white. As history unveils, we see that story over and over.

Hopefully, we will begin to eliminate the lie of race and racial purity. There's no such thing. Then the other thing is the whole false issue of—critical race theory is not the problem. The problem is, let's just tell the truth about our history. And I think—no, I don't think—I know that the truth will set all of us free. I love the story of freeing—emancipation just didn't free the slaves. It freed the slave owner, because they had to watch us and keep us from escaping. If you had, like, I think the estimates on the Stroud plantation was, oh, approaching three hundred slaves and twenty-five white people. The children of masters by those slave women who were taught to negotiate, to read, to write, to—as they called it, cypher, to count money—because plantations were little, small city-states.

My sense—from spirituality—is that you cannot erase the history. You cannot erase what actually happened. You can put pretty words on it. The name of the Brazos River. It's the arms of God. It's the Arms of God, the Brazos de Dios.

I grew up walking to Saint John the Baptist Catholic Church at the end of Faulkner Lane and Dallas Street, because it was a

Catholic church and because you could dance. In high school, we had dances at Saint John the Baptist—it's an interesting name for a Catholic church—in the basement. I later learned that in—learned this at the University of Texas—that the reason Texas became a republic is because a mestizo president of Mexico became president and he outlawed slavery. And so, slavery ended at the Brazos River. If you crossed the Brazos River, you were now in Mexico and you were free.

I also learned that the basement of Saint John the Baptist Catholic Church was one of the last stops on the Underground Railroad. You know, Harriet Tubman and all of that. But Mexico was a whole lot closer to Louisiana, Alabama, Mississippi, Arkansas, and Texas than Canada. That mestizo president outlawed slavery and told the slaves that if you come to Mexico, we'll give you some land on the border. In my college days when I first went to Mexico, I was shocked that there were people with a darker complexion—more melanin than me. Someone gave me this book—this story about that experience. From 1836 until they joined the union in 1846, Texas was its own empire, because they didn't want to do away with slavery.

I think that as time progresses, it would be beneficial if the Baptist power elite would embrace these true historical facts. I think that they're going to have to. But that formed the basis of my perception at a young age of right and wrong, good and evil, and a God. I just—I can't trust a God that I'm supposed to be afraid of. I can't trust a God that is going to punish me. I believe in whatever higher power is bringing more humanity to humans—to the other side. The loving, forgiving, compassionate, generous, totally unbiased, accepting everybody as an equal. Because if you're a child of God, we all are supposed to be equal. I had—that was my philosophy at, I don't know, twelve, thirteen. In my lifetime, I've explored religions to see if they fit. None of them do. I've read the Book of Mormon. I've read—of course, of course, I've read the Old and New Testament. I've read the Catholic Bible. I've read the Egyptian Book of the Dead: The Book of Coming Forth by Day, or, as they call it, the Book of the Dead. As

I was reading things, I loved reading the mythology and the folk-lore of all cultures. That's why Dr. Lovin thought I would be an excellent philosophy professor. I was on my way to being Angela Davis, go to Yale, major in philosophy. But Stevie Wonder said, "God knew exactly where he wanted me to be placed."

Part 2
Story

Does disaster befall a city
unless the Lord has done it?

   —Amos 3:6

Then the Lord answered Job out of the whirlwind:
Where is the way to the dwelling of light,
and where is the place of darkness,
that you may take it to its territory
and that you may discern the paths to its home?

   —Job 38:1, 19-20

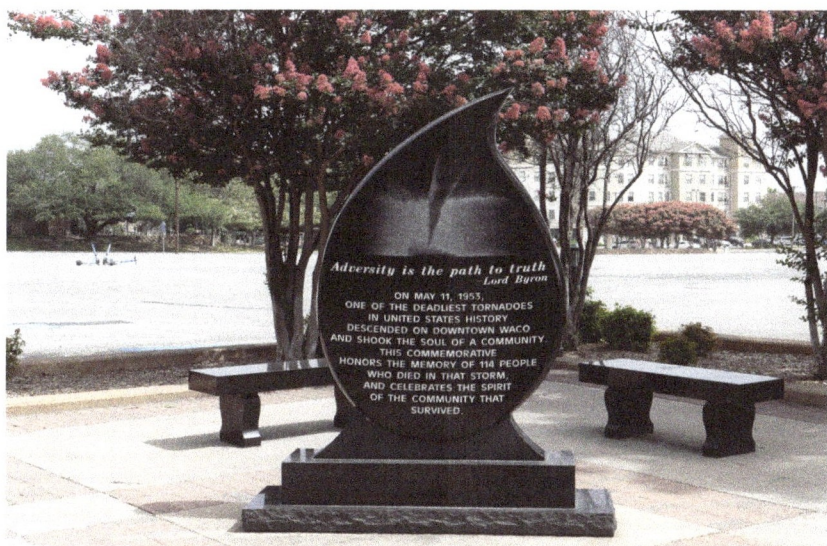

Adversity is the path to truth
Lord Byron

ON MAY 11, 1953,
ONE OF THE DEADLIEST TORNADOES
IN UNITED STATES HISTORY
DESCENDED ON DOWNTOWN WACO
AND SHOOK THE SOUL OF A COMMUNITY.
THIS COMMEMORATIVE
HONORS THE MEMORY OF 114 PEOPLE
WHO DIED IN THAT STORM,
AND CELEBRATES THE SPIRIT
OF THE COMMUNITY THAT
SURVIVED.

3

Michael D. Babers

Michael Babers grew up in Waco, Texas, before attending college in Austin and becoming a teacher. Babers recounts becoming active in political life in Central Texas, first with the NAACP and later with the Community Race Relations Coalition (CRRC) in Waco. Learning about the lynching of Jesse Washington only after leaving Waco, Babers discovered in his own family memories of the lynching and an oral tradition that connects the lynching to the tornado. Impacted by these memories and stories, Babers has devoted himself to works of remembrance, acknowledgment, and truth-telling.

I was not born here, but I got here as soon as I could.[1] I'm the son of an army veteran who was just discharged in the earlier part of 1968 and was on his way back to this area because he and his wife—my mother and father—were both from this area, near this area. I've been here in Waco since I was about three months old. I graduated high school here in Waco and attended college in Austin. I moved to Austin when I was eighteen years old in 1987. I lived there for around fifteen years. I took that long to find myself and figure out what, really, I wanted to do.

While there, I took a ministry route and became an ordained Methodist minister. I finally figured out what I wanted to do as far as a vocation. So I stopped working, went back to school at an HBCU on the east side of Austin called Huston-Tillotson College at the time (now it's Huston-Tillotson University). After finishing there, I started my teaching career as an elementary school teacher. Not long after that, I got very sick. I had already been diagnosed with Hodgkin's lymphoma. This was my second bout with it, where I couldn't really take care of myself like I needed to. My family was here, so I was invited by my parents, very strongly, to come back home. I have been here in Waco since that time.

I've been teaching elementary school—mostly third, fourth, and fifth grade. I've been pretty active in political life—mostly yellow dog Democrat. That's because my family was, and I decided that that's what I would pursue because they helped my community. I was a member of the NAACP there in Austin, so I would join here. When I got back here, there was a group that met weekly who had conversations concerning race. I really didn't understand why they were having the conversations when I first got here. But I soon learned that it was more of a cross section of people from different groups with different ethnicities. They would have conversations about what was going on here in Waco and how they felt about it.

At the time, the organization didn't really have a name. There's some backstory to this. It happened before I—the first person in my family to be involved in this was my father. Then, they had another round. Six months later, they had another round where I was chosen to be a part of this conversation. I was really interested. I was like, "Okay, what are you going to do with this?" So, I delve into it more. This is the reason they were having these conversations. Baylor University—at the time, George W. Bush was president of the United States. He had his "home away from home" in Crawford, just outside of Waco. He was considering putting his library at Baylor. Baylor met with the City of Waco to see what they could do to make Waco an attractive place for George W. Bush to have his library. As they were figuring out what was going to make Waco more attractive, they came across a stumbling block: Waco's reputation. In order to find out what Waco's reputation was, they had these conversations with people—all across the city—of different ethnicities to find out, what do we need to do? Or what exactly was there about Waco's reputation that might sway President George Bush to have his library here? The one thing that kept coming up was the lynching of Jesse Washington in 1916.

That began a group of people, who were selected out of those people who were in those conversations, to have what is called the Community Race Relations Coalition—to see what we could do to rehab the city's reputation. Because not only was this reputation built on that oral story, the picture of this lynching was featured at the Lorraine Motel in Memphis, Tennessee, where Martin Luther King Jr. was assassinated—which is now a museum. That picture is mentioned—is prominent there in that museum. It says, "Lynching in Waco, Texas, 1916," with a lot of smiling white people in nice hats as this body was hanging above a fire on a tree. So, this group was formed so that it could rehab Waco's reputation—so that we could be in contention for George Bush's library.

One of the ideas about rehabbing would be an apology, first. A reconciliation. An apology with real feeling about this, because Waco had not really ever faced this. I mean, it was part of our history, but nobody in the city had ever made an effort to say, "Okay. Yeah, this happened in our city." We also had the David Koresh thing that happened a couple of years earlier. So at least we could work on this part. We as a group came together and wrote a beautiful resolution and apology—reconciliation—over this heinous act that was done in our city. We presented it to our city leaders and our county leaders.

At the time, we had on our county commissioners' court a man named Mr. Lester Gibson. He was our first and only Black male to ever serve on the commissioners' court. He was the only one who was working with us and the only one who was actually for the resolution. After we wrote the resolution, we called for city leaders of all races and creeds to come together. Some of our most prominent people came together and read the resolution. Our resolution was rejected by the county commissioners. They said it was starting something that they had nothing to do with. Their people were not ready to do this, because they didn't have anything to do with it. They didn't want to start an uproar in their community. We even got pushback from leaders in our Hispanic community not wanting to do it. We ended up presenting it to our city council, who took it, watered it down, and said, "This is the one that we feel more comfortable with," which was pretty much—not exactly what we wanted to say, but it was something.

We decided, "Okay, well, we're going to keep pushing and this group needed to continue on." We were then—like I said, we chartered—we became a group here in the city. We started having annual meetings. Well, not annual meetings, but invited other people to be members. Those of us who were in that first group, we became board members. We have lasted from that time until now. Now, I'm an ex officio member, because I can't be as active as I'd like to be—not able to make in-person meetings at this point. But that's how we started. That's how that whole thing came to be.

Since then, we have made inroads with—we had an author from Dallas come to Waco and do research, and she wrote a book called *The First Waco Horror*,[2] Patricia Bernstein. We met with Patricia, and she was like, "Yes, you all have to do something—build a memorial or something to this—because this did happen." It gave rise to the NAACP in New York City, because there was a young woman from New York who was a reporter for *The New York Times*, who came to Waco and did a story on this. But she was white. Because she was white, she could ask all the questions she wanted to. They gladly told everything she wanted—everything she needed to know. She took that back to the NAACP, which was comprised of both white and Black members. That anti-lynching theme was one of the core principles of the NAACP, starting at that time in 1906. It had far-reaching implications. Waco was not just known here, regionally. Waco was known across the country for this lynching incident, so it wasn't just this.

Our local Race Relations Coalition has partnered with both—our Hispanic Chamber of Commerce, our Central Texas African American Chamber of Commerce, and our NAACP have all championed, been right there with us in our latest work. Our city has also come and partnered with us in a much more aggressive role. After we petitioned the state, we now have a memorial marker which is beautifully written. It is not on the courthouse because our courthouse is still comprised of those same people, minus Commissioner Lester Gibson, but then by his administrative assistant, Ms. Pat Chisholm-Miller, who was our first Black female commissioner. It's going to be in Heritage Square next to our city council, where the city council meets, next to the Convention Center. We had it all ready and planned out. When it arrived, it was broken. Somehow in the shipping, I think, it was damaged. It was broken at the point where it would sit on the pole. That part was broken. And so, we had to send it back. We were thinking about getting it repaired, but it wouldn't be repaired enough to really be sustainable. So, next year, we will erect that.

The cause became more noble than to just get a library. We knew we weren't going to get the library because once we started we were met with resistance. I mean we had an ancient relative of the woman who was murdered come to one of our meetings and actually confront me. I was wondering, Why me?—but, I guess, because I was sitting closer to her—about, Why am I digging up something that happened a hundred years ago? She told me that lynching was a form of punishment for those days. "He was as guilty as sin." I'm looking at her like, "Okay, you were there a hundred years ago and so you know that he was guilty?"

When the whole—The whole story is that the young man was mentally challenged. The guilty confession was based on a written confession that he'd made under duress in Dallas, deprived of sleep, with the mark of an X. Then, shortly after the verdict, they—the lynch mob—came and got him out of the jail cell, took him up, and strung him on a tree. He wasn't hanged. If he were hanged, we wouldn't have this conversation. He was lynched. He was taken out of the cell. He was burned. He was hanged. He was shot. His genitals were cut off. Fingers were cut off, toes cut off. Then, he was dragged throughout the city. That's lynching. That's a whole lot different than hanging.

We had a lot of work to do. And it wasn't something that we should stop. Because we wanted Waco to be better than this. We see it now in our—the way Waco stands, even in our state. You see places that are comparable to Waco, size-wise—Irving, Odessa, and Amarillo—places like that, who have about the same population. Those places are—the margin between Blacks and whites, as far as income gaps, are very much different. There's such a split—more so in Waco than there is in any other city.

Growing up in Waco, the entire Jesse Washington story is not one that is told. It's told in—it's one of those things that is told in hushed tones, not really vocalized. People just don't talk about it a lot. I didn't find out about the lynching until I was in college in Austin. A friend of mine from New York City told me. He asked me where I was from. I told him, "I'm from Waco. It's just right down the road." He said, "How far down the road?" I said, "Well, about a hundred miles." He's like, "Okay. Now I know I'm talking to somebody from Texas, who says a hundred miles is right down the road." But he said, "Waco, that's where they lynch people, right?" And I'm looking at him like, "No. Not really—" He's like, "Okay, I know I saw it somewhere." So, he went and found it and showed it to me. I don't remember what it was—it was a Black publication—*Ebony* or *Jet*, something like that. He showed me the picture. I was like, "Wow."

I remember coming home. My great-grandmother, who had been a resident of Waco pretty much most of her life—at the time, she was in her nineties. Well, she lived to be ninety-seven. She was alive at the time that the lynching happened. She was born in 1910. I asked her, I said, "Mother, did you know anything about this Jesse Washington lynching?" She said, "Yeah, they did it. Because they dragged him by our house." I said, "Wow. They did?" She said, "Um-hm. They dragged him by our house." She said she'd never forget that. She was a little girl, and they were playing. Her mother called her and told them to come inside so that they wouldn't have to see it. She, being the little girl that she was—she got in the window. She looked outside the window. She could see him as they were dragging him around the house. I was like, "Wow, you saw that?" She said, "Um-hm. Um-hm."

I asked another friend of mine who has relatives here in Waco. I said, "Mother said she saw them. She saw them! She said they drug him through her neighborhood." They said, "Yeah, that's what they said. But you know what else happened?" I said, "Well, what else happened?" They said, "That tornado in '53? It went the exact same route as they drug him through the town of Waco." I said, "Really?" They said, "Ask Mother if she knows about that." I didn't ask Mother, but I asked my grandfather. My grandfather was—he and my grandmother got married in '53. They got married in September of '53, which was after that—May the eleventh, I think the day is. He said, "Yes, it did. It did. We all did—we all knew it happened. We thought to ourselves, Well, we had been wronged once, but we weren't going to be wronged again, because the Lord got vengeance for us."

Then, I started asking some of the people who I went to church with at the time. They were like, "Yeah, that happened." They said that everybody who we ask says that same thing. It went the same way. The Black people felt vindicated. They felt helpless to do anything to help him as he was drug through the city, but they felt like God vindicated them.

I think that goes with our theology. That mixes in with our heritage, because a lot of times we are undervalued—and not being able to fight or stand up for ourselves at times. But if we didn't have our faith to draw upon, to know that God would continue to fight our battles and to vindicate us—we don't have that type of representation, that rock that we can go to. We don't have a—even today, we don't have a whole lot of political power anywhere else that we find through our religious faith. So, yes. That has been the subject of a whole lot of conversations.

So much of our history and our heritage has been lost. I have—my mother and father both were born at home. They didn't have birth certificates. When I go to the—find the records of their birth certificates—I see their birth certificates. I look at the time when they got their birth certificates. It's at the time when they would have been entering their first year of school, because at that time, they didn't need birth certificates. And my grandparents—not at all. Not until they got ready. Most of the time, the records of their birth that I find looking for them would be on a census record. I think that oral history should be passed on. We've got to have those. When we can get them and write them down, it's important. It's important to pass them down. It's important to talk to each other.

Some things are very painful to remember, which is why they don't get talked about. My great-grandmother didn't want to talk about it that much, because she saw it. She witnessed it. It's not something that she would want to relive all the time. There are some other things that, on both sides of my family—my mother and father's side—that they don't really talk about that happened in our family. Things that I think I should know. But they just don't talk about. I've heard that they happened—I might have heard through a cousin or an aunt or somebody else—but they don't talk about them because they're painful to relive. But somehow, they've got to get to the next generation. So, oral history is so important.

This story reminds us how evil unchecked will bring about a result that you really don't want to have. You really don't want it to be left up to God. It takes a heartfelt apology and repentance from evil and bad intentions for us to grow together and for things to be good. Because if you don't, you sow a negative seed that will grow into something that will be harmful for everybody.

That's how I see it. That's why we still have times when we get the community together and we celebrate Hispanic American heritage. That's why we still celebrate Asian and Pacific Islander heritage. That's why we still celebrate African American heritage. We need to keep those conversations going so that you can understand one another. Because if you understand and you're talking, then that leaves no room for hate. You understand one another. You talk to one another. Then it kind of clears up some misconceptions about each other.

May 16, 2006, is the day that we read that resolution on the steps of the courthouse, and there were a hundred people that were reading it. I think you'll see what we were attempting to do and why we felt it was important. I think we need to—as a Race Relations Coalition—need to go back to that every now and then, just to see. I don't know if you can see this, but these are two of the people who are—that's our new county commissioner. I don't know who that other lady is. But that's how moving it was, just reading it and having all of the city leaders there, from bankers to pastors to just ordinary people—community leaders. All of us were together that day and we read it. I think, you know, like I said, that resolution stated our desire and purpose for what we were doing. It's important that we go back, remember, repent. So that we can move forward. To me, that, more than anything else, can be a blueprint for what we need to do to go forward.

4

Bettie V. Beard

Bettie Beard offers powerful recollections of her experience of the 1953 tornado as well as experiences of racism and segregation in Waco. Beard also reflects on the many different stories she encountered as a child, including the whirlwind story. While such stories can be appreciated in their context, Beard believes that today it is more important to focus on the historical facts about Jesse Washington.

The tornado was an experience that I can't forget because I was a kid who was always nosy.[1] But I also had what they used to call a photographic memory. I say that because, as a little baby, I would tell my mother about things that I remembered. She would tell me when it happened and would say, "How do you remember that?"

During the tornado, it impacted me a lot because my mother was not home when the tornado hit. What I do remember is when my mom got home, we had been under the bed. But before the tornado hit—you know how you get before a storm comes . . . ? This was in the afternoon. I can't forget it because we had this big front porch. You could see all the way up the street. You could see from house to house. We saw lightning hit an antenna up the street.

We were at 700 Morrow Avenue. We were right in the center of Morrow, right before you got—well, it was two houses down from the creek. This was in North Waco right off Eighth Street near Waco

Drive. The first street you're going to come to on the right is Morrow, but you're going to come to Barron Avenue on the other side of the street. So, we were at 700 Morrow Avenue. We were outside, as we always were, because we pretty much lived outside. If we wanted to watch TV, we would go across the street because our neighbor had a television. She invited the kids, and she would always pop popcorn. All these kids sitting around on her floor, you know, eating popcorn and watching this little old television screen.

But this lightning that day, when it hit, my aunt was outside with us. Sometimes she would take us outside while she would clean or iron or whatever she was doing in the house. She would leave us outside to play. Well on this day she was out on the porch with us. She saw it. Just all of a sudden, it was like pandemonium. She said, "Get in here, get in here, get in here!" She put us all—there were two beds in the middle room—under the bed. At the time, there was my baby brother, my older brother, then three of my cousins. So, there were six of us young kids who were there. After everything was over—it seemed like forever—my aunt was just acting strange to us. She was just—she was nervous. I know that now. I look back at how she was behaving. She went, and she just said, "I'll be back." My other aunt had come home from work by then. It was late, and it was dark. My aunt took off. She said, "I'm going to find my sister!" She left. And this is how I really found out about the tornado downtown.

My mother was coming from work and the bus lines were not working. Back then, you got your transfer. When you got downtown, that's where everybody changed buses. There were no buses running! The tornado had already hit! When I say there were no buses running—how could the buses run? People didn't have a way home. My other aunt had made it home. She was telling my aunt how scared she was walking home. The main thing I remember is about her being scared to walk across all of those wires that were down. People had to be really, really careful, because there was stuff everywhere. She worked close to downtown also. My mother and she worked in different places. My mother told us that she went to the Medical Arts Building. I learned the name of the building later, but that's where the story—the folklore, some of the embellishments, and all of the things—began to happen.

My mother wasn't aware of the extent of the damage because she was at the Medical Arts Building on the corner of Ninth Street and Austin Avenue, which was just one block away. The damage didn't go past North Eighth Street. When you go on up to the Medical Arts Building—it's on the corner of Ninth Street and Austin Avenue, one block away. The wind was powerful, but I'm talking about the type of damage that they had downtown—the destruction that was just a block away. They didn't have that type of destruction right there on Ninth and Austin Avenue. I always knew where it stopped because my mother was relieved that she walked that way—and was able to get into that building. Now, there were stories in the community that were passed around, because you had Black people who were in the tornado, just like my mother on the bus. You had to get off the bus. Well, now you find yourself down on Sixth Street in all of this craziness. It's dark, and the storm is here. You want shelter, but they don't open the door at this building, or they won't open the door at that building.

When I got older—what I learned is that—we didn't understand racism. We just knew that there was a division. You knew that there were ways that we lived. You knew what you could do and what you couldn't do, where you could go and where you couldn't go. I didn't think of it as racism, I thought of it as segregation: "You don't belong here, you belong over there." They were not allowed into the buildings like the Orpheum Theater. Well, when those people who were in the Orpheum Theater died but the people who were outside lived, some Black people would say: "This is God's way of telling y'all about how wrong you've been, how badly you're treating us."

Same thing happened a couple blocks down. There were people who were in their cars—people getting out of their cars to go into buildings—and they were killed. Then, I heard that some people who were outside in their cars survived. But some cars got crushed. Because we walked downtown and saw the destruction. On the square, which is where our history really was, we heard about how devastating the tornado was. We frequented the Mecca Drug Store.

We knew that the people who had the meetings—the funeral home was downtown. You know, the dentist was downtown—Dr. Garry Hamilton Radford Sr. was downtown. I knew about that later. I didn't know about that then, because we didn't go to Dr. Radford. But Dr. Radford went to New Hope Baptist Church, so we knew him from the church. We found out he was there in the tornado when it hit. He was upstairs. He survived that tornado.

There's a lot of stories that people have told over the years, you know. Our coach had a son, Lewis Richardson, who told me he and his mother had walked downtown. They lived in South Waco someplace between Ninth and Tenth Street. Lewis had told me that the day of the tornado—he and I were the same age, I was less than a week away from my birthday when the tornado hit. The tornado was on May the eleventh. How can I ever forget it? My birthday is May 16, 1948. I was getting ready to turn five years old when the tornado hit. Lewis would share with me the story of him walking with his mom, because he loved being able to have that alone time with his mom. He had one brother, but it was him and his mom—not him and his mom and his brother. He said they walked home. As soon as they got home, the tornado hit. Lewis said that the fear that he always thought about was, "My gosh, if my mom and I hadn't left and gone home when we did, what would have happened to us?" I can't imagine what happened to some people who were walking. We know that there were people in their homes who died as a result of the tornado. We also know that there were people who died in their homes when the tornado hit. It hit East Waco pretty hard.

The other story, the main story that they tell is more folklore than anything—because the path of the tornado may have included this path that people are talking about, but that was a very short area. When they talk about the lynching of Jesse Washington, they say the tornado went down that path and followed the path of them dragging Jesse Washington. Because they drug him beyond—after the lynching—they drug him all the way back out to Robinson Drive. So, it doesn't even make sense. The story doesn't make a lot of sense.

This story was everywhere. It was too bad, because, again, it was supposed to be biblically referencing: *when people do wrong, this is what happens. This is God's wrath and because of the lynching, the tornado hit Waco. The tornado was never supposed to hit Waco. The story was, we were in a valley. We were deep in—the tornado could never hit us. But God brought the tornado here because they lynched Jesse Washington.* I'm thinking in my mind—I'm a kid. Later on, I'm putting two and two together and saying, "Wait a minute. That lynching happened way back then. The tornado happened in '53." I mean, if it had happened a year later or a couple of months later, then I could see. We knew we were listening to myths. We knew we were listening to myths.

There was another story that said the tornado landed in the middle of the Brazos River. We were little kids. We'd be walking to the park. We'd walk over to Bledsoe-Miller Park some days, which was then called Doris Miller Park. Those were our outings. We would do hikes. We would do picnics. When you're walking with kids, they say, "Well, my parents say the tornado stopped right here." You listen to kids. It's just all kind of little stories like that. You knew better. Even though you were in elementary school, you knew better. That story about the lynching—we didn't have the name as kids—the Jesse Washington name wasn't out there. It was about the lynching. I wasn't even that much aware of the story until I became an adult.

I think that it was just a coincidence that the tornado happened to travel down the square and into downtown Waco in the Austin Avenue area. If you look at the actual path of the lynching, Jesse Washington was taken from the courthouse toward the bridge but they turned around and went to Waco City Hall where he was lynched. They did drag him down that path—down that direction. But that was a short few blocks. That tornado went on for miles. The destruction path was wide. Naturally, it could include that one street, you see. I wouldn't be so foolish as to ever believe that, although I still say there needs to be a reckoning.

I think that history shows that there was doubt on all sides when it comes to the lynching. The beautiful thing that happened right after the lynching was Baylor University had a front-page story with an apology for the horrific, dehumanizing treatment of Jesse Washington. As a Christian school, they knew it was the right thing to do.

I knew the story that my grandfather told, and I still don't know which lynching he referred to. But when my grandfather first moved to Riesel, my grandfather, being a sharecropper, came to town to sell his wares. He always came to the square. On the day that my grandfather came to the square in his wagon, he had one of my uncles with him. He witnessed the beginning of a lynching. He didn't witness the lynching. He witnessed someone dragging a man. I don't know how many times, because I'm sure it's more than once that the dragging occurred because of the nature of the people who lynched at that time. When I say "the nature"—the human nature—we're still trying to become civil. We still have a certain level of civility that we still need to work on, so you're always dealing with that. That day my grandfather left without doing any business. He turned around and left. My grandfather didn't tell us this story. This was told by my aunts, mother, and uncles later. They were talking about it one night when I was sitting at the table.

They talked about how my grandfather went back and said, "I will never go into town without my knife again." My granddaddy just felt like he wanted to always be able to protect himself. But I knew that it was probably true because of what I witnessed with my own eyes when I was a teenager when I went to Palestine with my grandfather and saw that he carried a knife with him.

So when I look at that and I look at my granddaddy coming to town on his wagon—feeling like, "Wow, I'm helpless. I'm helpless"—and comes back to town. Every time, he's coming back without his protection. He didn't like Waco. That's why he wouldn't move into Waco for years.

We still didn't get it. We never knew about segregation. We didn't know about segregation. We lived a good life. We had our churches, our stores, and everything. We didn't have anything missing. We didn't know or understand segregation even when we went to the Rex Theatre. It was integrated, but you went upstairs. You were sitting on these bricks. I thought this was the way that theaters are made. Years later, I understood. There were no bathrooms up there. I began to understand as I got older. But we didn't know about segregation, so the stories that we heard—they weren't that powerful. They weren't stories that hit you and you said, "Aha! This is what happens if you do this." It wasn't that.

I don't think many Blacks in our community understood segregation because we lived a certain life. Segregation was something that—if you lived up North, you're going to be much more aware of what you can do. Everybody was busy living their life. What was missing? This is what I'm saying. The inequality is what was missing. A lot of people in the South accepted segregation because they didn't pay attention to the inequalities. It is because of history. Once they were freed, that became so very important—the freedom. Northern Blacks had always had the freedom to go to school— integrated schools—to be educated and to learn to read. So now, you can finally learn to read. You can go to school. You can purchase homes. It was different. When I talk about that, I'm not saying that it didn't matter how you were treated, because we were aware of that—you were treated differently. If we went to the stores, we were going to be followed. We didn't understand the mindset. It was like, "Why are they following us?" Well, we thought, okay, they think we're going to steal something because we were Black. That was it. But as far as the why—not understanding attitudes—we thought white people just didn't like Blacks. It was just simple like that.

As I said, the tornado story was myth. You can't find anyone who won't—I don't care where they live. They can live in Houston and never have lived in Waco but just have connections to Waco. They can live in California. They can live anywhere, because that folklore circulated. But again, it's myth because the tornado tore East Waco up. The tornado hit my friend's house who lived in an area close to what we call Frogtown. Their roof was damaged really bad. Their mother was in the house and in the bed, trying to get comfortable. She got really soaked. She got pneumonia. There was a lot of water around. It flooded. She died. She didn't get the help she needed. Another friend lived on the north side near the river banks. Her mother was killed in the tornado. The tornado was blind to race.

But what we know is, down in that building on Fourth or Fifth Street, a lot of people got killed. I know there was a Black man who worked in there who was related to one of my classmates. He got killed. So, the tornado didn't have a target, saying, "Okay, we're going to kill all the whites and leave the Blacks." It didn't. So, I'm just saying. That's why the myth is just what it is. It's a myth. Most people—I don't believe that most people really believe in it now. If you are truly—if you're an older person that believes that you have to pay for your sins, then yes. You're going to believe it. You can't take that away from people who are connecting the tornado to someone's mistreatment of other people. You can't change what people believe.

I'm just saying—among family members. You may not think that even your young family members know the story. But everybody knows. It's only that tornado because they mention the lynching in Waco. It went down the path. People have circulated that for so long. It's just that because when we were in school, not one of our teachers ever said something like that to us students. Once it starts, it builds and builds and builds. It's just a rolling stone. That's all that it is. It just keeps gathering, gathering, and gathering moss, right? It's just a rolling stone that gets bigger and bigger, and more and more embellished. What I wish they would focus on is—if they really wanted to do some [good for] folks. Nowadays, with all the DNA, you know—there are so many things that should have been done years ago in terms of trying to find out. Not many Blacks that I've come into contact with believe Jesse Washington was guilty. They felt he was simpleminded and it was easy to paint him as guilty. He was an innocent guy who took the fall for someone who chose to kill this lady in the way that they did.

My grandmother loved to tell stories. She would tell us to do this, do that—and why you do it. We had limitations set. For instance, you don't go up on Colcord Avenue. You don't go on Ninth Street after dark, because you didn't belong over there. We lived on Eighth Street, one block over. We went to Ninth Street when we were little kids to get snow cones on the corner of Ninth and Morrow. But you're not over there in the evening. My grandmother loved to tell us stories to teach us to be safe. For instance, you don't go up on Colcord Avenue after dark because you didn't belong over there. Stay in your neighborhood. We lived in a mixed community of Hispanics, Italians, Germans, and African Americans. We frequented their businesses. Occasionally we would play with them on the playground.

My grandmother worked for white people. She was a domestic help. Sometimes, they would bring the kids over to our house. We'd play with them. We didn't see race and we didn't realize how wide the gap was. We played with them but we didn't go to school with them. Nor did we go to school with any of the kids in our neighborhood who were not Black.

Our schools were segregated. One of the things about our segregation was that we always had to use old textbooks. We knew that our textbooks were old because you didn't have anyplace else left to write your name. So many other students had had it before you. You got handed down those textbooks, but you didn't have a place to write your name. If you wanted to keep your book together, you had to put a book cover on it because they were falling apart.

And there were other little things that were frequent reminders that we lived in a segregated community. It was going to McCrory's and S. H. Kress & Co., knowing that you could go in the stores. But those stores had fountain drinks. You had to go to the back. Then, they wouldn't wait on you until they got ready. You could sit there for an hour, and they didn't have to take your order. Those kinds of things. It was going to the bus station. It's hot. You've walked all the way to Bledsoe-Miller Park. You're coming back from East Waco where—just a block or so from home. But we're going to stop at the bus station because we're hot. We want some water. You go to the bus station. You turn on that little white fountain in the coloreds-only waiting room. The water barely comes out. I wouldn't drink water because it was hot water. Once these places were integrated, for the first time, I tasted that cold water from that fountain. Oh, that was a major impact. I saw hate. I see little kids coming in. They're hot. At that time, we were young. We could go to the park on our own from the time I was seven, eight, nine years old. We could go to the Gem Theatre. We all went together—my cousins, my brothers, and I. We could go all the way over to the Gem Theatre.[2]

We didn't begin a struggle for justice until years later. Trying to replicate what others were doing in different communities wasn't meaningful or impactful. For instance, sitting in at the counters. Waco didn't have it as bad as other places. Oh, there were problems. We had a hootenanny downtown. I will never forget the time that a Black man got too close to the door of Piccadilly, and the whites converged on him, thinking he was trying to go in through the front door. That's how territorial people were. This is why I can understand the attitudes of people during the tornado not letting Black people in the buildings—because it was a territorial thing: "You don't belong here. You can't come in here."

That's how I—that's just my own interpretation. Looking at the history of Waco as I experienced it, again, people weren't cruel in terms of you walking down the street and someone's just going to attack you. Now we had a lot of times where we were chased by young white boys. They'd be driving down the road and we'd be walking home or on our way downtown. White teens hung out downtown when we were growing up and we lived near downtown. They'd get out and start chasing us but never really tried to catch up with us. You get too close to Cameron Park—we played on First Street a lot—you get too close to the entrance of Cameron Park, you're getting chased. One time, we actually got chased all the way through the park.

But I'm just saying, I didn't see segregation in a bad way—but I felt the brunt of it as time went on. As we got older, we felt it. You didn't see it as much as you felt it. You're paying more attention as you get older to the way you're treated. When you're a little kid, you're not paying too much attention. You say, "Oh, this is our neighborhood. This is what we have to do. This is what we were told to do." When you're eating in the back room of a little small restaurant, you don't think about it. But you're sitting back here—years later, you can remember that you had to sit among boxes in a storage area at some cafés. My mother worked at a cleaners when I was a little girl, and she took me to work with her one day because she needed to take me to the doctor. When it was time for lunch we went across the street to eat in one of those back storage rooms. You don't think about where you're eating at the time.

You don't think about the difference because you're not up front. You don't see it. But you become more aware because you have this memory. You become more aware of the surroundings and how you were treated. You become aware of being told that you can't come here, you can't do this. But nobody ever tried to correct things like someone not waiting on you or the waitress taking forever to wait on you. Who cared? You either got up and walked out and never went back, or, if you really wanted that food, you had to wait. That was the kind of thing we experienced regularly.

Segregation hit us harder in our schools. When I got older, I was very aware of it. I was aware of not being able to go to Waco High. I was aware of our books. I was aware of some things that were going on in the community where it seemed like we weren't getting opportunities that others were getting. Our library was super small. Then, finally, they integrated our libraries when we were in junior high, and we could go to the library on Austin Avenue. Our small library on North Sixth Street was closed and moved to East Waco in the early sixties.

When we went to the library downtown, we weren't treated badly at all. We were always helped by the people at the reference desk. I can't say that the downtown librarians knew more than our librarian on North Sixth Street, because I had a close relationship with Mrs. Wilson. But, I appreciated the fact that the downtown library had the reference books downstairs. All those reference books! Books I never heard of before. I started getting serious research assignments when I was in the 7th grade that continued throughout high school, so I appreciated all of the books. Oh my gosh, so many different books. I had a limited number of books on Sixth Street. I love books. I could not believe that there were so many books and magazines in the library. You could go in there and read magazines all day long.

So, the library wasn't segregated, but guess what? When I graduated from high school, I put an application in to work at the Waco Public Library. I was told that I didn't pass the test—the very simple test. I was an A student all my life in English. They couldn't fool me. It's like, oh, they didn't have to show me the results. They just told me I didn't pass the test. So, when I moved to Houston, it was such a different feel. Not segregation, but I knew that what I had experienced in Waco had been racism. When I moved to Houston, I applied for a job at Foley's department store which required a test. I was hired immediately for an accounting department supervisor. I mean, it was an immediate hire—a different feel from Waco job opportunities for Blacks. I loved math! I was good in math. And I had been typing since I was in the seventh grade. So, those same skills and knowledge that I had when I applied for jobs in Waco got me that Foley's job!

But the Waco librarian told me I didn't pass the test. Same thing with—was it Citizen's Bank or First National Bank? They told me I didn't pass the test. Math test! That was my forte. That was me all day long. They told me I didn't pass the math test. I'm this person who never took out a pencil to use scrap paper on any test. All my life, I never did. I mean, this is what was happening. That wasn't segregation. That's racism. That's what I was being exposed to as I got older. I began to see racism in Waco. It was very ugly, because you got lied to. There were doors that were closed. There were certain jobs that you could not apply for. But one man was very honest with me when I applied for a position. He told me that if I went to another city, I could get this job. He would recommend me. But he told me that Waco Chamber of Commerce had a lot to say about who became manager in this area—I didn't even realize. When he told me that, I didn't know whether to believe him or not. He could tell me anything.

I began to see racism and the way that people were promoted, the way they were treated, who was hired, our administrators for the school district. We had some very, very brilliant people at our school but for some reason, not one Black person had been hired as an administrator until they closed A. J. Moore High School down. I don't know if they did this as an accommodation or what, but Principal J. J. Wilson and Coach Vernon Hicks from A. J. Moore High School were hired as the first Black WISD administrators. Those hirings were a good thing. You don't think about that when you're in school. It wasn't so much about segregation during those times as it was the inherent nature of racism in Waco.

When it comes to the question of my upbringing in the Waco community, I remember that we had what I considered a closed community even if we did frequent common spaces and common businesses shared by all Waco residents. We grew up in happy spaces being comfortable frequenting our neighborhood stores, barber/beauty shops, churches, schools, funeral homes, etc. But everything started with and was strongly guided by family. Family traditions and family values were respected. You have to realize that what people did—they looked at their life. How they grew up. They shared stories based on their belief system. A lot of people didn't have education. My granddaddy's education was, like, sixth grade. My grandmother was similar. But they were very, very engaged. Especially my grandmother. My grandmother was always watching the news. She was always writing letters, communicating with her family, and visiting her family. So, she was always sharing stories. As a child, sometimes you'd hear things and you'd say, "I don't believe that." Or, you know, you'd hear different things—and you'd believe it or not.

You trusted your older people. You listened and you believed, pretty much whatever they said when you were young. Whatever they said—you didn't think of it back then as folklore. You thought of it as the truth. If they told you something, why would older people lie to you? You weren't allowed to lie. That was one of the sins. You couldn't even say the word *lie*. We'd listen to little white kids, and they could use the word *lie*. We couldn't! Even telling stories, you just didn't do it. You might get your face slapped if you so much as said the word. So, we trusted. Now, that doesn't mean that we didn't have some uncles and cousins that we knew were telling tall tales. We began to understand about how people embellished. We couldn't say, "this is folklore." We looked at all the stories in a different light based on where we were in our understanding and our interpretation. But again, some people—if they talked, you weren't listening to them at all. Because they had a reputation, right? "Oh, here comes Uncle Sam. He's going to tell us some more lies, y'all."

So, they loved to tell you stories. You didn't know what was true and what wasn't. We got a lot of stories. They weren't related so much to, like, the lynching and the tornado. But you also had stories about East Waco—when people began to move to East Waco in large numbers, some people would say, "Oh, they're going to drop a bomb over there because of all the blacks"—you know, stuff like that. "There's too many of y'all moving over there." By the time I was in junior high school, this type of talk in our neighborhood had died down because East Waco was growing and thriving and it was the place to experience a lot of positive activities. There was an influx to East Waco in the fifties also. There were new homes built—new additions built in the fifties. It was nice. We talk about racism. It's like, "Okay, we can get land over here, but you can't get land anywhere else." We didn't look at that. Nobody even thought about that. We were just glad to have new homes being built. That's not folklore. It was just the truth. It was a fact. They make this available. You can go over there. This is what's been made available for you.

As we talk about the Jesse Washington lynching—I can't help but think of George Floyd. There have been many horrific incidents before George Floyd, but this public killing by a police officer pressing his knee on Floyd's neck in such an evil way played out all over the world. People saw it. They were sickened by it and said, "This is not me." But if you just read about it—and you don't see it before we had all these cameras—you can look at it and say, "Oh, how terrible." You can move on. But when you have these images seared in your mind—and these images are coming on television, *on every channel, every day, all day long*—how can you, as a Christian and as a person who even cares—even if you're not a Christian—how can you look at something like this and know that it was so very wrong? It's like, how can this happen? You have people standing all around. You have this one guy, the policeman, who is killing this man and won't let up a bit. No one would intervene.

That to me was a major, major fault of people—who we are, why we're afraid to intervene, why we're afraid to go toward him. Was it that gun? I mean, surely the other policemen wouldn't take their guns out and fire at you if you went into—I still don't get it. I don't get it. To me, it was the same thing with the Jesse Washington lynching. Just heinous. Then, they burned him alive. Burned him and did a slow burning. Would take him up and drop him back down until you heard him scream. The whole thing—when you think about this horrific nature of this young kid who was accused and then given a quick trial with no one to even attest to his character and his behavior.

I go back to that. I look at George Floyd. I look at all the different excuses that people can have for not doing anything. There on the square around Waco's City Hall, thousands of people—they came from all over. There was a picnic. They couldn't get close enough. They were joyous. They were desperately taking parts of his body on the way to and from the lynching as tokens.

I would never sit around my living room or at a party and discuss the tornado story connecting the tornado to Jesse Washington with anyone in this day and time, because we know that it is foolish. I'm saying, today, to have a discussion on the pros and cons of it—Was this right? Was this not?—we know better. We don't have to have that discussion. But I would not want to take away from the understanding of people who lived in that time, who had experiences that they couldn't help but relate to that. It's like, "Oh, see what happened because of how you treated us? You see what happened?" They believe that! That's why I say it would be foolish to talk about that incident other than in a historical context, because we don't have to discuss pros and cons of it.

Now, to discuss the pros and cons of what happened during the lynching—that's more important. Don't focus on connecting the tornado to Jesse Washington. I don't care about myths or folklore—I care about what happened with the destruction of Waco by the tornado.

As far as connecting the tornado to Jesse Washington, I think that what's more important is that investigators continue to focus on analyzing the case and seeking additional facts regarding who could have killed Mrs. Lucy Fryer—we want to have the facts, okay? According to Jesse Washington's family and some research articles, questions remain about his guilt. We've never had all of the facts.

Never had them.

5

Nona Kirkpatrick and Anthony Fulbright

Nona Kirkpatrick and Anthony Fulbright share what it was like growing up in racially segregated Waco, recollections of the 1953 tornado, and thoughts about how racism continues to shape the present. Kirkpatrick speaks of traumatic memories of lynching that for a long time were held in silence in her family. Her grandmother shared these memories with her family during the tumult of integration. Fulbright summarizes the spirit in which such memories were shared by elders as an "unwritten thing that we're going to tell you, because we're looking out for your safety." The failure to overcome racism and to value people over profit informs Fulbright's closing reflection that today "we're in for a revolution."

Nona Kirkpatrick: I've lived in Waco for seventy-six years.[1] Growing up in Waco, Waco was rigidly segregated racially, but everybody had their own space. You didn't cross over into anybody else's space. I didn't find it a problem till, well, later years. I realized how unorthodox this was. I attended a newly built elementary school. It was Kirk-Wilson Elementary School. I started school in September 1952. It went to the sixth grade. Then, I started junior high at A. J. Moore High School. It went from seventh through the twelfth grade. Everything was separate. It never was equal. It was separate. But we had excellent teachers at A. J. Moore. I feel like we had a chance to progress. Most of the kids came from two-parent homes, then. At the time, life was good to me. I thought life was good. I attended church—St. James. It wasn't United Methodist then. It was just St. James Methodist Episcopal, I think.

Anthony Fulbright: I grew up at 1605 South Third Street in Waco, Texas. Our household consisted of my grandmother, my grandfather, my mother, me, and my dog. My daddy was overseas, fighting in World War II. Everybody in the place where I grew up was African American, Black, whatever you want to call it. I attended the Church of the Living God right over here on Church Avenue. My granddaddy was a pharmacist. My mother—my grandmother was a preacher. She became disabled and got where she couldn't go on a walk. But she could still get out there and whip me, for some reason. I was nine years old when my mother went back to college. My daddy sent her to school. She went on to get her bachelor's degree at Paul Quinn College and her master's at Texas A&M University. I went to Kirk-Wilson Elementary School—I was a year behind Nona—and on to A. J. Moore High School, where I thought I was probably one of the best athletes at the school—which I was.

I graduated in 1965 from A. J. Moore and went to Sul Ross State College out in Alpine, Texas, for two years. Kind of got injured, came back to Waco, and enrolled at Baylor University, where I got my bachelor's and my master's degree. The day I walked out of Baylor, I went to work for the American Red Cross as director of safety and disaster services. I, too, witnessed the tornado, because I was standing in the window, and my grandmother made me get out of the window. I worked for the Red Cross for thirty-six years. I came back to Waco to retire. My mother and dad were both getting up in age. I felt like it was best for me to come back here. I'm an only child, so I felt my place was to come back and do what I had to do. I paid the price with the space I occupied, being an only child. Had to take care of my dad and my mom.

Kirkpatrick: The thing I remember about the tornado—it got dark in the middle of the day. I was in first grade. I lived a couple of blocks from school. It got real dark, and my mom came to the school to walk me home. I was kind of mad, but I did what she said. When I got home, it started thundering, lightning. I was always afraid of lightning, so I got on the sofa. She had a way of covering you up that you would go to sleep if she covered you up. She covered me up. I'm the only person I know who slept through the tornado. Because we lived in some little cardboard—it wasn't cardboard, but—little, tight army barrack apartments. She said she just thought any minute they were going to blow away, but they didn't. When I woke up, we couldn't turn the lights on or anything because the electricity was out. She had a coal oil lamp because she was raised in the country. She lit this lamp, and I thought that might be fun. After a while, you get tired of that.

People started dropping by. One of the neighbors had been in the movie theater. The Black movie theater was the Gem Theatre. It crashed, and she came home with all this debris in her hair and everything. She was lucky enough to make it out of there, because I don't think some of them made it out. People started talking about the destruction downtown. Oh, it was bad for a long time, because—for a long time, if it got cloudy, I just panicked. My mom wouldn't let me go down there. Some of the neighbors went down there.

Fulbright: My high school was on First Street. My elementary school was on Second Street and Third Street. I lived on Third Street, right down the street over the bridge, which was—Waco Creek used to come through Baylor. I'd go—you know, I'd just walk home every day. That particular day, I walked on—you know, it looked like, to me, that God had a way of raining in the morning. About time school was out, it would quit raining and we'd walk home. It didn't just seem like that to me. So, I got home. My mother got home. My dad was working out of town. I think he was—must have been in Corsicana or somewhere, because he built dams and stuff. He was a constructional engineer. Yeah, because he had gotten home from the military—back from the war.

It started raining, and it was raining, and then it stopped raining. It started lightning and thundering. Then it got dark, like, darker than a hundred midnights down in the cypress swamp. It was dark. So, I went to the window. I was upstairs. I went to the window, and I looked out. My grandmother came up there. She said, "Boy, if you don't get out of that window—!" So I got out of the window because, you know, you do what Grandma says. So, I got out of the window. Grandma said, "And just come on downstairs." I came downstairs. We were all, kind of, downstairs. All of a sudden, it was over. The sun came out. It got just as clear.

My mother comes up with this wild-eyed idea. She said, "I need to go to the post office and mail my brother a letter." I think it was his birthday coming up or something, and she wanted to go. The only post office that we knew back then was on Eighth Street and Franklin Avenue. That's where we wanted to go. So, we got in the car [. . .] and we headed down to the post office. When we got around Mary Street, we realized we couldn't get to the post office. When my mother turned around and we went back home, I heard her trying to explain to my grandmother what was going on, and my grandfather. We didn't realize the damage. The thing that always stuck out to me was that Amicable Life Building. I had some pictures. That sucker kind of swung both ways and stood straight back up. Everything around it was gone. The tornado came through there and wiped out Bridge Street and everything down through there—where they tarred and feathered the guy that got hung.[2] That tornado took that same path down through there. You bet you—I mean, it went straight down Bridge Street. From the river—that bridge that's still standing down there—but it went straight down through there. You know, I'm a little boy. I hear Mom talking about it. I'm going, "Oh, man, I want to go down there and see that." And it was—our lights went out, but everybody had—not a Bunsen burner. What were those things?

Kirkpatrick: Coal oil lamp.

Fulbright: Coal oil lamp. Everybody had coal oil lamps whenever the lights went out. I finally managed to get down there. I think my grandfather carried me down there. I saw devastation that was unbelievable. There was a train station on Mary, because there were two train tracks there then. Nate Chodorow's Dry Goods Store was right here, so it's behind Nate Chodorow's. That would have been Second Street and Mary where the tracks—this big train station, it was leveled. I don't know how many people passed away, but it was leveled. The two things that I know remained was the Amicable Life Building and Raleigh Hotel. Everything in the middle was just torn up.

I didn't realize the devastation being—it took me years to read about, to realize exactly what happened—because that was the square. Right in front of the square, right across the street from the square, is Waco City Hall, just like it is now. That sucker came right down through there, dodged all of it, and went right on down through there. A little damage in the square. That's where all the Black guys hung out and laughed about where they were going and everything. It was a bunch of—I'm going to say juke joints and beer joints and what-have-you and pool halls. Over here was the Mecca Drug Store, and right down from the Mecca Drug Store was the Gem Theatre. Then, you got to First Street. Then, there was debris, and it went on. Everything over here on this side of town was seemingly all right. But everything was—oh, man. It was awful down there. The post office was not harmed. The Amicable Life Building wasn't harmed. The Raleigh Hotel wasn't harmed.[3] Everything in the middle of it—just demolished. Here's City Hall. In City Hall was the city jail. No damage. That tornado came right on through there and went straight on down Austin Avenue, wiping things out.

Kirkpatrick: I heard the story of the lynching because of my mother. My mother and her siblings were really brought up to not talk about that—but they said that—because they dragged him from the courthouse and took him to that bridge that was built, the Washington Street Bridge. I think the bridge was built in 1903. This was in 1905 that the lynching of Sank Majors happened. They said a tornado went through that pathway. The story about Sank—my maternal grandmother, who was his sister, told that to me and two of my cousins when we were maybe about ten years old. I could tell it hurt her to talk about it, but she wanted to tell it.

So, she told us the story about what happened to him. My cousins were twins—they were boys—and what, I think what brought it on, it was about, maybe, 1954. They were just talking about integrating the schools, and my grandmother did not want that. She said, "I didn't raise none of mine up to go to school with no white people." You know, she said, "Don't you ever be alone with a white woman, because if somebody sees you, she will lie on you." Then, she told us what happened to her brother. My mother and her siblings didn't talk about it. But my daughter was in elementary school, and she found a book in the library. It had an article in it about Sank Majors. She came home and asked my mom if she knew him, because my mom always said we were kin to the Majors. Mom said, "Where did you get that?" She said, "It's in my book. It's in a book at school." I think she had brought the book home. She talked about it that one time, and she didn't want to talk about it.

When Patricia Bernstein contacted me—I told my mom about it—she was coming to Waco to talk to me because she was going to write a book. My mama got on the phone, called her sisters, and told them. She said, "Some white woman is coming to Waco to talk to Nona about Sank Majors. You know she'll tell all her neighbors about it." Patricia Bernstein wanted to talk to them, but they wouldn't talk. They were afraid for me to talk, because they had been brought up to be so afraid of talking about it. They didn't know what the people would do. At the time, I was—I had a job working in Marlin, Texas, for the Texas Youth Commission. One of my aunts said, "You don't need to do that, because you know you have to go down that highway every day to work. These people have probably got relatives that still live there—you don't know what they'll do." I said, "Well, they don't know what I'll do, either."

Fulbright: You know, that story stays the same regardless of who tells it—because I didn't know anything about it. You remember when the Brazos River changed course right down there? You know where the Doris Miller Memorial is down there now? That was where the Brazos came through. Shortly after the tornado, the Brazos just moved over about fifty feet towards downtown. You know, because, where—that's where Bledsoe-Miller Park is right now. That's where the Brazos River used to be.

Kirkpatrick: I think I do remember that. I was a little girl.

Fulbright: It was an unwritten thing that we're going to tell you, because we're looking out for your safety—but don't you say nothing. Don't you let anybody ask you anything about it.

Kirkpatrick: That was it.

Fulbright: It was just another unwritten rule, you know? We went out to Majors Chapel Cemetery and tried for the longest time to figure out where Sank Majors's grave was.

Kirkpatrick: Nope, there was nobody living that knows where he was. He was buried at that cemetery, but nobody—they didn't mark the grave or anything, because—

Fulbright: Why would they?

Kirkpatrick: They thought that white people might come and dig up the body, because the day after he was lynched, his brother, Curtis Majors, came to Waco to claim the body. They had some kind of little rinky-dink train that ran between Waco and Golinda, wherever it was—

Fulbright: It was called Interurban—whatever they called it.

Kirkpatrick: Yeah, well, they shipped the body back off—they took it out—what was left of the body. They took it out and buried it in Majors Chapel Cemetery.

Fulbright: We spent a whole day down there. The thing that I picked up on—because they were kind of filming her. I was just there, because I didn't have anything to do with it. I'd just gone out there with her. There is a section out there that's blocked off and fenced off. You can't get in. I just concluded in my head that he's probably buried somewhere over in there. I couldn't prove that to save my life.

Kirkpatrick: And I hate I didn't ask my grandfather. I was only about ten when my grandmother passed away, but I was a grown woman with children when my granddaddy died. I hated I didn't ask him about that and ask him where Sank was buried, because he was one of the people who helped bury him. But at the time, I wasn't thinking about anything like that.

Fulbright: This is a guess, but it probably originated in one of the old Black barbershops, because barbershops had beauty salons with them.[4] If you wanted to find something out, you'd just go there. You could hear all the stories you ever wanted to hear in there.

Kirkpatrick: Yeah, probably.

Fulbright: That's probably what happened. I can't prove that, but there used to be a place right here, right next door—this used to be H-E-B. This used to be an actual H-E-B store, and then two blocks down the street was the Safeway. In between that was a place called—what was the barbershop?

Kirkpatrick: The Jockey Club.

Fulbright: The Jockey Club. Anything you wanted to know, you could go in there and find out. Now, it sounds funny, but those guys weren't lying. They could tell you what was going on.

Kirkpatrick: They sure could.

Fulbright: Who was that guy that wore the tight blue jeans?

Kirkpatrick: Mr. Gentry.

Fulbright: Man, he knew everything. I don't know when he died. He just kind of faded away. He'd come in there sometime and he'd say, "You know, y'all don't know nothing actually about what happened down there when Majors got hung, do you?" Then he'd kind of sit there and kind of chew on that old cigar a minute till somebody would ask him. He'd say whatever he had to say and then he'd walk on. But he knew it.

Kirkpatrick: The peculiar thing about Sank's lynching was, they had just a kangaroo court–style trial that probably lasted thirty to forty minutes. But he had a real attorney. Now, Sank's people didn't have any money, so that wasn't why he was doing it. But this white man, back in 1905, put his life on the line to defend him. The Ku Klux Klan threatened to burn that man's house down with his family in it, so he asked for a change of venue. He must have had good reason to ask for that, because it was granted. But it was a hot summer night, and the more beer that the Klan drank, they decided that it wasn't going to be any change of venue because they—well, they didn't break down the door at the jail, because the jailer said he had just got a new door. He wasn't going to make them break it down.

Fulbright: Oh, he let them in. That's just borderline.

Kirkpatrick: Yes, so he let them in. That's when the lynching started. I think it's in Bernstein's book. She provided me with some copies of newspaper clippings from back in the day, too. It was all—oh. In fact, the *Waco Tribune-Herald* finally printed me an apology of sorts for their part in it, because every day, they started their article about Sank as "the black beast" and "the black brute." They were very racist. They did finally apologize.

They didn't take Jesse anywhere to kill him. They killed him on the courthouse alone. But they dragged Sank from the jail down to the new bridge that had been built in 1903. That's what people tell me: the tornado went that way.

Fulbright: "The moving finger writes; and, having writ, / Moves on: nor all your piety and wit / Shall lure it back to cancel half a line, / Nor all your tears wash out a word of it. / And that inverted bowl they call the sky, / Whereunder crawling coop't we live, we die, / Look not to it for help—for it / as impotently moves as you or I."[5]

"But I will lift up mine eyes unto the hills, from whence cometh my help. My help cometh from the Lord, which made heaven and earth."[6] That's what I go with. Sometimes things just happen. When we're just coming out of the Pentecost—and here we go. But I honestly believe that God punished Waco for the hostilities that they brought down on it.

Kirkpatrick: Oh, some evil things—

Fulbright: The evil that they'd do lives with them. "The good is often interred in their bones." That's *Julius Caesar*. It was just amazing that the majority of the Black people that were downtown during this tornado didn't get harmed. I told you that Bridge Street stood up. All the buildings on Third Street—they were still there. The Mecca Drug Store was still there. The Gem Theatre was still there. But the Fox Theatre got torn up, right down the street.

The Waco Hippodrome Theatre down there got torn up. Then it just went straight on down Austin Avenue. The more I looked at it, the more I've read about it, and the more I've thought about it—"But for the grace of God, go I." Something happened there that I don't think any man on earth could predict nor actually be able to write correctly about. That's just my—I shouldn't have said that, but that's my thoughts.

Kirkpatrick: I guess it may have been about a week before we went back to school. I was in the first grade. This little girl who was in the second grade, her daddy had a tailor shop—I think it was a cleaners and tailor's shop—down on Bridge Street. Every day after school he would come, pick her up, and take her down to his shop with him till it was time for him to go home. Well, he had picked her up that day. She and her daddy were killed in the tornado. That was because—well, you know, when you're in first grade, you don't have friends who are dead. I knew what cemetery they buried her in. But somebody finally showed me. Somebody finally showed me her grave. She and her daddy. Well, her mama's dead too, now, so they're all buried together there.

There were a lot of innocent people that died during the tornado. So, I don't—on the one hand, I said it was this—one hand, that. But I don't really have an opinion of that.[7]

Fulbright: After the tornado. And M. Lipsitz & Co. Ltd.—I don't know if you know anything about Lipsitz down there—the junk, people that buy junk. Lipsitz was downtown on Franklin Avenue—on Franklin and First Street. When the river moved over, Lipsitz moved over too. They moved across the river to over here. They're right down the street here now. They're getting ready to move, I think, from down there—out on Loop 340.

But it's just amazing. Now, I just have to believe that this is going to happen again in Waco. I've seen it happen twice here in my lifetime.

There's a guy who is a friend of mine. His name is Donny Keezee. He lives on Orchard Lane. Please don't call him in, because he has a hard time dealing with what I'm about to tell you. Donny's son never came home one day. Donny was a local mail carrier before he became the postmaster in Waco.

Kirkpatrick: He was my mailman.

Fulbright: He was the mailman. His son got up one day to go to school and did exactly what he did every day. He never came home.

Kirkpatrick: To this day, he has never come home. That was back in the eighties.

Fulbright: They found him in an old refrigerator. Dead. We all know that that boy would have been valedictorian of his class out in Bellmead at La Vega. They found him dead. Tornado came through there. Did the same thing out in Bellmead. That was, what, about the eighties?

Kirkpatrick: Yeah, that was in the eighties.

Fulbright: Yeah, storm went through that same path. Donny's still alive. He and his wife. That was his only child. Oh, man. We know what happened. The path that this little boy, little Keezee, would have walked. Ran right through there—you know, where he went every day to catch the bus to go to school. But this guy—same thing happened in Bellmead, where that path—or something near that path—tornado went through them. Wiped those guys out. We knew it was the Klan. We couldn't prove it. Nobody could prove it. I saw Donny one day down in the Fifty-Fourth District Court trying to get any judge to—what could he do? He needed proof. He couldn't do anything. I don't know the boy's name, but I know his daddy's name was Donny Keezee. He's still here. He's out on Orchard Lane.

Kirkpatrick: They say if you don't know your history, you're doomed to repeat it. I think people should know what went on in Waco and have something to compare it to—if it's improving or not. I can see improvements, and I can see places that still need some improvement. But that's the way that I see it.

Fulbright: Well, no. I will, though. I added something on Facebook a few days ago that got me to thinking: you know, we are doing the same thing over and over. It's all hate. What's going on now kind of reflects back in my—to my way of thinking—through home training. We can't seem to get along with each other. Why? Is it home training, or is it hate? Well, if you're teaching people to be hateful, they're going to grow up to be hateful. That's kind of what I see ahead of me right now.

Kirkpatrick: Like the Maize shooting.[8]

Fulbright: Yeah, that's ridiculous. What's going on? Then you've got somebody in authority who is more interested in his back pocket or his pocketbook than he is in the life of another human being. I'm talking about the House of Representatives, Congress, and anybody that would vote against a gun bill.

Kirkpatrick: Don't leave Donald Trump out. He's not in authority, but he's trying to get back in authority.

Fulbright: Well, all of it is not Trump. I think that we're in for a revolution, I believe. But the time to revolutionize is going to depend on what we do as a people, not necessarily what the House of Representatives or Congress does. Goes back to home training.

Part 3
Spirit

What winds came
when we prayed, those of spirit
or hurricane?

   —Will Wellman, "Haiku after Irma"

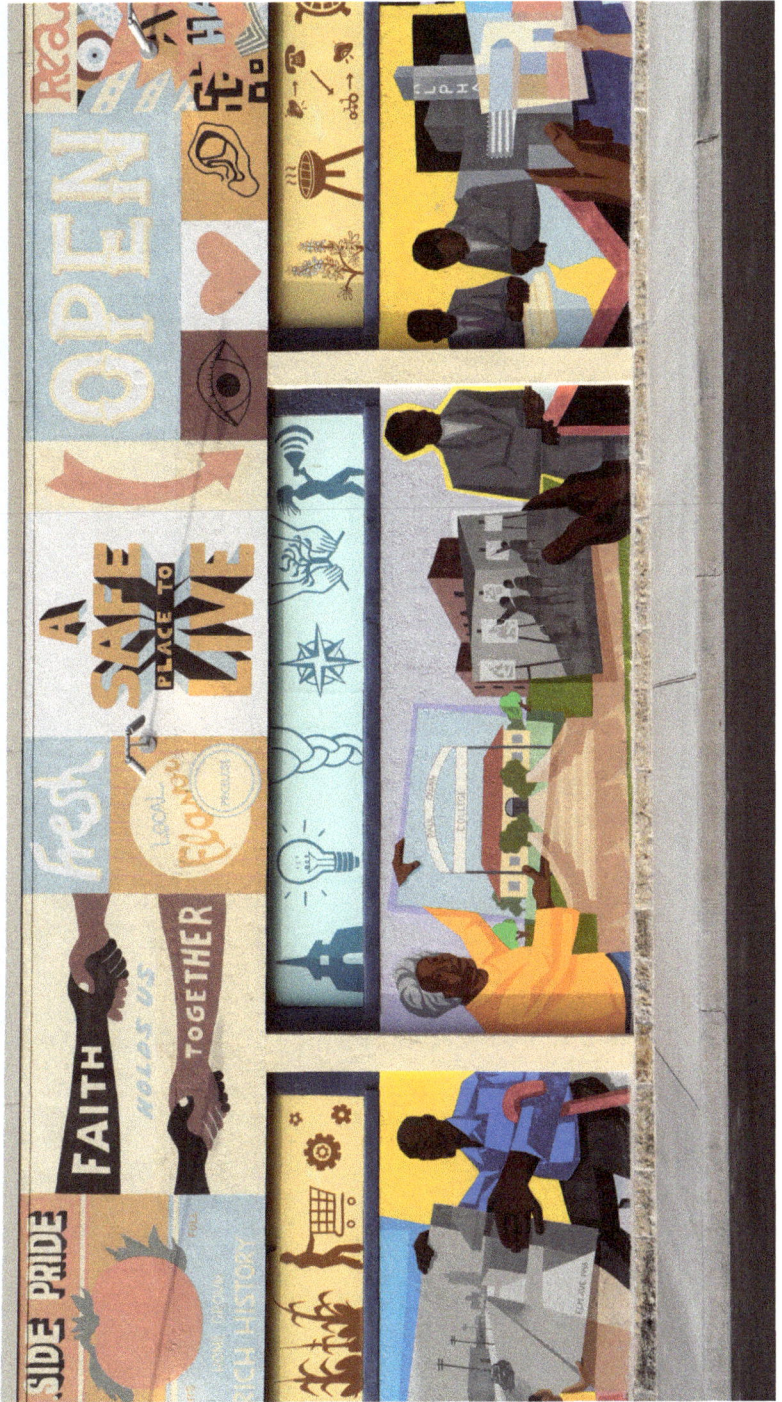

101

6

Ramad D. Carter

For Ramad Carter, life in Waco has always been a whirlwind. Growing up, Carter experienced the richness of being part of life-giving and sustaining community, the hard-earned wisdom of his grandmother's protection, and racism on the street and in the classroom. Carter reflects on his own activation, an awakening that took place after learning about the history of the lynching of Jesse Washington and the whirlwind story. He discerns in the story the protection of ancestral magic. Having experienced consciousness-raising power in such stories, Carter considers the difference sharing stories can make as well as his sense of responsibility to uncover other stories that have been hidden from view.

I am a born Waco, Texas, native.[1] I've been here pretty much my whole life. In the year of 2012, I moved to New York City, where I got my undergraduate degree in Dramatic Arts at The New School. In June or July of 2020, I actually moved back to Waco, Texas, where I started my Master's of Science in Early Childhood Education and Teaching at the University of North Texas. Waco, I came back.

Growing up here, I would say, what really comes back to my mind, as a kid, I remember—it was kind of one of those cities where me and my friends rode bikes all around town. I remember I played basketball barefoot. But it was Waco. This is what we do. I just remember community. I grew up in East Waco. I moved to North Waco my freshman year of high school. A large portion of East Waco—and if you're from Waco, [you know] there are different parts of Waco that are very different. It's like if you go to any other town. We have East Waco, North Waco, and South Waco. I grew up in East Waco for elementary and middle school. My high school years I spent in North Waco, which was from my freshman year until my senior year. It was a big change, because East Waco—and this is just how I would put it if you were from here—it's a little more hood, you know. It's a little more rough around the edges, you know what I mean? But I feel like everybody was still a family. You knew everybody that was on your block. My grandmother would go eat across the street with Wanda, they were best friends. I was best friends with her daughters and all of their friends. It was very communal and very family oriented.

I grew up in a Mexican household, so that was very interesting because, traditionally, my grandmother had a lot of cultural references to Mexican heritage. It's how she grew up. It's funny. Growing up, I didn't get to go anywhere. My grandmother was kind of one of those skeptics, you know. She had lost two children to violent acts. One of them, she lost at fifteen. By the time we reached a certain age, like fifteen, my grandmother got so strict. She was like, "You're not going anywhere. I don't want you out late at night." I really felt like as a kid, I was very restricted on the things I could do [. . .] But it's just the culture and the life I grew up in. I think it kind of affected the way that I saw—or kind of how I really valued family and friendships and my relationships that I had with people because of the way that my grandmother structured how we grew up. It was very important. Family was very important. Relationships were very important.

High school resembled the communities of Waco. We were very cliquish. They were—I mean, to me—and this is, from my knowledge, tended to be very racially divided. I know that there was a lot of issues between Blacks and Hispanic people. That was the biggest one of all. It's kind of crazy, because it didn't even involve white people at all. Blacks and Hispanics were the ones that were always violent with each other. From that point, moving there from East Waco, which was more of my hood experience of Waco, and then moving to North Waco—which, to me, it was more like middle-class. If you go from East Waco, Olive Street, to Colcord Avenue—Thirty-Third Street and Colcord, there are larger houses, more middle-class.

So, I would walk around those neighborhoods, and I'd be thinking about how—there's somebody that's in this big house right next to us. You know what I mean? It's a different world, and I didn't realize what that meant. I've never experienced any hardship as far as race or anything like that. I remember leaving high school one day. I think the first time I even had an experience or an encounter like that was when someone drove by in his pickup truck and called me a "n—." Like, just yelled it out of the truck. I just was so shocked, because I was like, I've grown up here my whole life and I've never heard anyone call me that. It just really threw me back. It's so funny because I never experienced that in East Waco. I never experienced that there. I never heard anybody call anyone other names. It was a predominantly Black community, you know what I mean? So going from this family-oriented life where I had all these friends and then going to North Waco where I didn't know anyone—[but] there were [some of] my friends that went to Waco High that lived in those neighborhoods. But I didn't—they were so spread out, versus East Waco, where everybody was right here, you know what I mean? It was just very—it was a culture shock for me.

Even just moving twenty minutes away to a different part of Waco was such a culture shock for me. But that was the first time that I remember as a kid where I was like, "Wow, somebody just called me that. That's crazy." I never forgot it. I actually never told anyone about that, because I just kind of put it in the back of my mind. But it's funny because if anybody would ask me about Waco when I moved away, that was the first thing that would pop up in my mind—that somebody had called me that. Because they always say, "Is it racist? Is it racist?" And I'm defending my city, because I'm born and raised here. So, I'm like, "No, this is not how we do things. It's not like you think it is." But then I'm like, [whispers] "Somebody actually did call me that."

It was crazy. It was very much like being between a rock and a hard place—actually saying it out loud makes me really sad. Because even working with the students here in Waco and things like that, it's just—they need love and kindness and support. Sometimes it's just so absent. I felt too, as well, that that was a lot of my growing up in Waco. I was not really a social kid per se. My friends would kind of just force me to go into these groups and circles, but I did see a lot of that. Even when I saw white people at my school, I was like, "You go to my school? Why would you want to come here?" You know what I mean? This is Waco High. It's kind of insane. But that's kind of, like—I don't know. My experience in Waco—it was very, like, kind of minimal in just these major instances that took place and stick in the back of my mind.

I remember—fun fact is that I would, during the theater show—one of the shows that I worked on, and the name is leaving me right now—I had to play a slave. We were doing research on different stuff, so at that point in time, during that show, I read the Willie Lynch letter. That's when I first ever heard the song "Strange Fruit" by Nina Simone. When I heard the [song] during rehearsal, I walked in and there was a video playing on a big screen. I'm walking in, looking at multiple lynchings of different Black folks [and] throughout it there was a culmination of photos that had been put together to go with the song. Again, I really want to touch back—I never experienced that type of conversation, had those types of conversations, or saw anything that visceral, because I grew up in a Mexican household. There was not a lot of conversation about Black America and "This is your heritage," "You should look at this," and "These are the things you should do."

I realized I was a Black man—I felt, like, more so in that moment—me actually understanding what it meant to be a Black man in the world, in America and historically. I wanted to do more research. I got on a computer, and I got on YouTube. I started searching for videos of lynchings and stuff—just to learn more about what that was. There, I randomly played the one

[that] popped up, and it said "Jesse Washington." So, I clicked it. I was like, "Oh. I don't know anything about this story." As I'm watching the video, it said it happened in Waco, Texas. I was blown, because I had never heard of that story in my entire life. I didn't hear professors, teachers, anyone ever talk about that story. I'm like, "How? How have I lived my entire life as a Black man and I don't know about this?" I watched the entire video. I was like, "Oh, my God. This happened in Waco." Like, it happened here. Down—and it's like, I've been in downtown Waco. It happened in downtown. I still didn't know about this story. I've drank over there, laughed and played over there, and not even understood the history of what happened in that space.

I feel like once I started having conversations with people—because, of course, after I found out, I was like, "Did you know that someone got lynched in Waco?" I started telling other people about it, because I was like, "We, as Black people—none of us have—did you guys know this?" So, I started going around and seeing—and telling stories about him. I think I had come in contact with an older native of Waco. That's how I understood the association to the tornado. From what I was told is that it was more related to a supernatural act. The tornado happened because they were displeased—whoever "they" are—was displeased with the act that took place in Waco. My understanding is that the tornado followed the same path that Jesse Washington was drug. It destroyed that entire path. It may have actually been Ms. Linda Lewis, because I do remember us having a conversation about that.

I mean, for me, I'm a believer of many things, you know what I mean? I believe in spirituality. I believe in magic and things like that. I believe that there's different versions of that for different people. So, me knowing about the story, I'm like, "This is terrible. This is horrible. That [tornado] deserved to happen. Waco needed a wake-up call." I saw photos of the postcards that were made, in the slideshow. I was like, "I've looked at this building"—just to see people's faces, and they're still in my head, on the postcards, and his body there. It just—it's so—it's still stuck. That story, the tornado, seeing the video, and seeing the photos, it's still stuck in my head. Sometimes it just plays over and over.

When I heard it, I felt like Waco needed a wake-up call. I feel like it also made me think about, there's probably so much outside of that story that we don't know. When I think about stories of Black folks coming up missing and they can't be found—historically, I don't know anything about how that's taken place in Waco. But I highly doubt that that was the first time. I highly doubt that; maybe it happened and there were no stories about it. For some reason, that story publicly caught the nation's eye, but I really—something deep down in me tells me that's not the first time. I wonder about that when I'm walking through my city and my hometown.

The supernatural aspect of that—I really feel like there's so much residual energy of that incident. I feel like a lot of it comes from the fact that nobody talks about it. Nobody knows. There's those untold stories that also mix in with the ideas of the history of Waco that we don't know about. Because I'm like, "This is just one story. This is one small story that nobody knows about." I really think about that often. How many other times has this happened to people where nobody knows about it? I feel like there are graves, you know. That's just my opinion. I really feel like there's a lot more supernatural stuff within the city of Waco, outside of that tornado in relation to Jesse Washington. I don't think it's just because of that one time. I think it's people who haven't probably been put to rest, you know what I mean? So that supernatural energy is here.

I just think, like, the energy—I believe in ancestral magic. That's something that I believe is real. I feel like—even in theater, there were times when I was working on projects that were in relation to slavery and heavily involved Black work. I would sit and I would be like, "Ancestors, give me strength. Give me the power to portray this story of this person so that they're heard—that they're seen and they're visible." I feel like at Mission Waco—the Jubilee Theater there—I don't know. I feel weird sometimes in there. I know a little bit of the history of that theater, but I just also feel like—again, there's some stuff that we don't know in Waco. I feel it sometimes when I walk in certain spaces and when I'm in certain areas of Waco. I feel like—it kind of scares me, because I feel like we've covered up a lot of stuff.

I believe there's other stuff that probably has happened, that I associate with supernatural activity. But I believe in ancestral magic. I think that when you hurt Black people—African folks—you anger the ancestors. They come back for revenge. It may not be instantaneous, but at some point, that energy from that comes and manifests itself. I really believe that that's what the tornado was. I believe it was manifested energy of ancestral magic.

Because I felt like I was a weird kid, and I always was interested in stuff that other people weren't—I'm a little bit of a fraidy-cat, let's be honest about that. I'm not into ghosts and things. I've seen those type of apparitions and things like that, but it just made me a believer. And I will say, I'm a firm believer in God and Jesus—that's where I'm rooted—but I also do believe in ancestral magic. I don't think I can be a Black man and have seen the things that I've seen, or experienced the things that I've experienced, and not say that I believe in ancestral magic or that magic exists. It just made me more open to receiving things. I feel like I became somebody that was very interested in learning about people's stories. That's something that was super important to me. I made space for that. I made time for that.

I think it did have a lot to do with the fact that [snaps fingers] once I was activated and not knowing that. It's crazy to be born and raised in the city and not even know that somebody who looks like you had that happen to them. It just really opened my mind to really thinking about—questioning more. Like, having conversations with people more. I really started valuing the knowledge that older folks in Waco, or outside of Waco, were giving to me, because I'm like, "Bro, these are stories that people probably don't know" or "It may be your job one day to pass these stories down to somebody who may not know." I'm never going to not tell the story of Jesse Washington. I don't care who has a problem with it.

In my time going to McLennan Community College —I don't know where this man is now. I hope he's well. But I was in, I believe, a social—it was either a social studies class or social science. I can't remember. I don't want to remember that class. But I remember sitting in there and, ironically, the professor brought up Jesse Washington after I watched that video. Like, I'm talking about within the next week. This is what I mean about ancestral magic. I feel like that was destined for me to be in that classroom that was full of white people—and I was the only Black person in that class with a white professor. And this man said that what happened to Jesse Washington was right—it was the right act, because he had performed a crime and that he deserved what happened to him. I was sick. I literally froze in my seat because I was like, "You are my professor." Then I started thinking again, "How many times have you told people this? How many people have you said this to?"

So, you have people in Waco—in my hometown—going around thinking that this was actually an okay act. That's sickening to me. It was a lynching. And so of course, I literally—because I could not sit in my seat anymore—I literally stopped him. I was like, "Sir. That is so inappropriate. That is absolutely disgusting what you just said." He was like, "Well, what do you mean?" I was like, "Do you even know the story of what happened? Have you done your research? Have you taken the proper steps to be [sharing] that type of oral history?" There's two types. There's the kind that is true and actually carries on legacies, truths, and rights. And there's those oral histories that are being passed around that just are toxic, manipulative, and just hateful.

It really sickened me to sit in that classroom. I couldn't even look at him. I had to leave because I was just like, "I'm not staying here. It's crazy for you to be a professor in Waco and saying this." So, I was in disbelief. I was in shock. I couldn't believe that—again, I'm still processing emotionally what I just learned about my hometown, and I'm hearing someone say it in that light. It was a lot for me to process. I had nobody to talk to about it, because nobody around me was kind of like [a] conversationalist. They weren't people who really challenged ideas of that. I had to keep all that inside and process that by myself. I was just like, "Oh. Okay. I came in contact with a racist act in Waco." I was like, "Oh, well. Never thought I would hear it in college, but here we are."

I wasn't totally alone spiritually, but I feel like, coming up, there is still a certain amount of power that you get from being able to talk about it. Thank God for people like Stevie Walker-Webb, where I learned so much about Black culture, Black history. I was being challenged to think about who I was as a person, as a Black man, in my city, in my hometown; an existing product of my hometown and going other places. There was a lot of conversation that surrounded that. Me discovering that and figuring out how I'm seeing it valued in my hometown based on what I've heard my professors say. I don't know if this man was a Waco native or not. I didn't care to know, because I was done after that. I'm here working with Black kids, Black boys, Black women every day—and that's what I know to be existing. So, yeah, I feel like the ancestor leads me in certain spaces to be able to, I don't know, probably tell these stories to people who don't know. I just have random conversations with people all the time.

I feel like it's kind of become my responsibility. I know a lot of Black people are exhausted from that—always having to explain and having to correct. For me, it felt like that often for me in undergrad. I would say that once you know something, that's when you can't not address it. So, once I knew a little bit more about what racism was and how I had come in contact with it, I'm like, "Yep, it's your job to make sure that never happens again to you and to other people that are around you—or to anybody else in the world." I'm not going to talk about all the ways that I have dealt with that, because some of them are not very nice. But I feel like they were also still warranted and needed and necessary. Sometimes how you respond is not always thought through. I feel like it's my job, you know, to talk to the younger generation and tell them stories like this.

Sometimes you do that, you're like, "Why do I have to be the person to do this?" But then, I feel like it is my job. It is my job to—because I'm loving and I'm caring and I'm kind, I'm a nurturer, you know—to sit and tell little Black boys and little Black girls these stories, because you need to know about your history. Especially if you're here, born and raised, you need to be knowing about the things that affect you and your family. It's just my job to do that research, to push and have conversations. I learn a lot more through conversations anyway than—of course, when I learn something, I'm like, "Oh, did you know?" That's my thing. Then it branches off into a conversation with someone else—bearing that fruit and sowing that seed everywhere kind of activates not only me but other people around me, too.

I'm sad that I didn't learn about this in school. I'm going to be completely honest—I think it would have ignited a fire of wanting to engage in conversation but also creating community amongst other people in my classroom. I went to a predominantly Black high school. Like, why did I not learn this in high school? Why did I not learn this in elementary school? We're here, guys. I just wish that it would have been more embedded in education. It's such a fight to get people to talk about African American history, African history, or Black Americans in the classroom. Even outside of this Jesse Washington story, we have never talked about Black anything in my classrooms. In a predominantly white high school, we never talk about anything like that. I just really believe it's so important to be able to engage in conversation and share stories. I feel like—also you learn more about yourself sometimes when you hear stories about other people. Jesse Washington—hearing about Jesse Washington, a young Black man in Waco—that's me. I always say sometimes, I don't really think people really value or care about something until it happens to you. I feel like sometimes that's when you're so much more invested in making something happen and sharing something.

Lynching is not—it's not new. A lot of us know that in the world today, some of these things are still happening. There are multiple articles that I read that—some have been recent, some have been further back—where I feel like lynching is still happening. It doesn't make national headlines, but there are conspiracy theories of things happening—of mothers coming home to their sons hanging on the tree in their backyard. I think it's also for our protection. It's not just, "Yeah, this is what happened in the past," but also to be like, "You need to protect yourself. We have to look out for each other. This is how we protect each other." These stories prepare us for what's to come or educate us about the past, so we can be better human beings and learn how to really just look out for each other. Really invest in that sense of community and really supporting each other. I think it's super important to have oral history—whether it's past or present—to be shared around and amongst your community.

Your story is important. It's valued. It needs to be shared. The knowledge that you have is wealth. It's great for me to be talking about him, because I never thought that I would even have a conversation about him. But it's definitely innate in me to feel a responsibility to share this story with other people.

There's a complex conversation around what it means to believe in things, whether it be supernatural—whether it be, you know, religion-based. Even though those are your things and those are your rights to have what you want, I really feel like me telling people or believing that this is a supernatural act would really make a lot of people pause and freeze and be like, "What do you mean by that?" Or it could also become a conversation where I felt like if someone was a firm believer in God, they would have a rebuttal with that. They would talk about how magic and supernatural things can't exist unless it's good things. I believe there are both versions of that. How you see that story of the tornado could either be a good thing or a bad thing. I believe it was justice served. That's just my opinion of it. I don't feel bad about it. When I think about the story—watching those pictures and all those things like that—I'm like, "Waco, you deserved that. You probably deserve a lot more." That's how I feel. I probably wouldn't shout that—I probably wouldn't go to Waco City Hall and say, "You deserve a lot more, Waco."

I would say that I'm grateful to be a native of Waco. Everybody's story is so different. I didn't grow up in the sixties, so I can't [speak on] that experience of what that may have been for somebody in the sixties is definitely going to be different than my story. But how it affected me in the future—historically, finding out that information, and how it allowed me to transform as a Black man in Waco—it definitely had an effect and an impact on my life. I feel like when I mention slavery in general, he's the first person that I bring up, because that's relative to me. I know this story. It's from my hometown. It happened here. I'm knowledge-able about that. I feel like when it comes to conversations about that, that's the first person that I think of immediately. I feel like that's my duty. I have to share that. That's kind of my [job]. I think that's my soul tie to ancestry magic. There's a tie there whether I want it to be or not. It is just a tie there. There's a spiritual tie there. I just feel responsible and excited for these oral history sto-ries to be shared with other folks.

There's an image of one of the postcards that had hundreds of white people staring back at the camera, which is horrific when you're looking at the photo in the context of the actual story. It happened in a tree in front of City Hall. Every time I drive in downtown Waco, that image pops into my head when I look at City Hall. It's crazy. That's what I see every time I see City Hall.

And to be honest, it's kind of like when I call upon the ancestors—teaching me how to prepare me for a show that I'm about to get ready to tell stories of other Black folks—I feel like he's one of the people that ignites me, you know what I mean? He gives me that supernatural [boost], Jesse Washington. I feel like I don't know who I'm calling from Waco, that's exactly what I'm saying. When I say, "Ancestors, imbue me with courage and fear-lessness," I don't know who in Waco I'm pulling from or calling from or getting this power from, but I know that they're here. I know that they're present.

Something tells me that there's a lot of stories that just need to be uncovered and discovered. I even feel led to do more research on that myself. But there are definitely some folks that have some stories that need to be told here in Waco. It's the energy I feel. It's the energy I see. I really feel that it's important. It's that connec-tion, for sure. When you speak something—when I share that story of Jesse Washington, it's like he's activated. That story is activated. The curiosity in others is activated. It's becoming alive. It's an actual thing that is being spread around and in Waco—the place where it needs to be. It has a tie.

As a Black man, actually touching that, sitting in that classroom as the only Black man, and having that [moment] feels like a supernatural lynching. That's what it feels like. It feels like I'm being smothered around a sea of white folks who just feel okay to falsify stories and not have any respect for the fact that there's a Black man sitting in front of you. And you still felt okay to say that? That's why I left. Because, why am I the only one opening my mouth? Why am I the only one saying that this is not okay?

And I looked around and watched other people just look back at me like I was wrong for having issue with it. It was like—it's not an easy journey—telling these stories, sharing these stories. There's pushback. That's why I feel like things like supernatural activity really have to propel you, because this is not easy stuff to do. There's a lot of people that you may meet in Waco who really feel like that story is okay—that it was right. They're not going to be Black folks. But I'm going to do it anyway. I'm a rebel. I'm going to tell the story. I'm going to tell it to every Black person I can. I'm going to be honest.

7

George Oliver

"Everybody doesn't look for meaning in the wind." But "prophets do." Reverend Oliver learned to look for meaning in the wind from his grandmother, especially from her spiritual practices of silence and from her knowing insistence upon reading the Bible, then by kerosene lamp, during Gulf Coast storms in Edna, Texas. Reverend Oliver additionally shares of his time in and with the Black Waco community, notably with Linda Jann Lewis. These experiences contributed to his dynamic interpretation of the whirlwind story—its persistence and significance—as reflecting the historical, theological, and cultural tapestry of Black oral and storm traditions.

In the grand tradition of Linda Jann Lewis, I stand as, I believe, a seventh-generation Texan, and a descendant of the Stroud plantation.[1] My roots in Waco go pretty deep. A lot of the African American population that is in the central part of Texas came from that plantation, which at one time encompassed around four counties. Up until about eight years old—which doesn't seem like a lot, but it was a very formative time, growing up in Edna, I was a member of Shiloh Missionary Baptist Church, which—Reverend Garry Roberts, Sr. (Father of Rev. Garry Roberts, Jr., Senior Pastor of Antioch Baptist Church in Waco) was my pastor and baptized me. He's now the pastor of Mount Sinai Baptist Church here in San Antonio.

Having worshiped in Edna, San Antonio, Waco, and elsewhere, I think that I've seen the traditions of our people lived out. One of the themes was this idea of the prevalence and importance of the motif of the storm in Black homes. I grew up, again, in Edna. It's in the Gulf Coast region, about a hundred miles south of Houston on Interstate 69, and we are closer to the coast. When there would be more southerly tropical storms or hurricanes, we would get these really powerful gulf storms. The lightning would be so many different kinds of colors. But any time a major storm came through, my grandmother pretty much had the same kind of tradition. It was similar in lots of other Black homes. She would unplug everything and make sure that the TV was off. Make sure that the radio was off. Like, there was nothing on. I remember she would light a kerosene lamp, because that's what the old folks used to do. Light a kerosene lamp—in case the electricity went out. But really, it was so that she could read her Bible. She would open her Bible, and start reading certain scriptures in Psalms sometimes. Sometimes it was even in Lamentations or other things. You'd know it was real bad if she was reading in Job.

As soon as the storm seemed like it was about to really start doing something, she would say the phrase, "George, be still while God is doing his holy work." Usually, the only choice was, go lay down and go to sleep, or sit still while God made lightning and thunder and rain and wind and all kinds of other racket that would come with these storms. I saw this motif pop up in some of the writings about the storms in—the tornado in Waco. That was the first theme—I was transported in my own memory to my ancestors and my family: the traditions—religious, deeply held religious convictions—that were more than just words in a book. These were "things." These were doctrines and principles we had to live out. So, where some people read of the scripture and—it's one thing when the Bible says, "Peace, be still," when Jesus is speaking to the storm[2]—this meant something to us. If it got loud outside, my grandmother would get loud inside and start praying very, very mightily.

For the first couple of years, my grandfather was there as well. Again, my grandmother's edict was universal. When she said, "Be quiet," everybody had to be quiet, including my grandpa. He wouldn't even pull out his guitar and start playing. He would just sit while she read her Bible. I don't know what he was thinking, but no one was allowed to talk.

My grandfather died when I was six. So, two years after my father died, my grandfather passed. My grandmother and I stayed another two years in Edna and then moved to Huntsville. I finished high school there. I finished elementary, middle school, high school in Huntsville. But the storm when we were—I say we were kids, because I feel more like a sibling to my aunts and uncles. But what I remember watching was, when we were kids, it was silence and the kerosene lamp. As adults, most of my father's generation, when they were moving into middle and upper age, it was no longer the silence. This was another generation's iteration: they quietly reflected. Or as the ancestors used to say, they laughed to keep from crying. They chose togetherness, unity. They used that time that they normally didn't get to spend together. It wasn't a family reunion. It wasn't planned. They talked about family and faith again like they used to.

The storm has a way of bringing the family back to a certain type of conversation—or at least provides that space for them. When storms come in family lives, not the actual storm, the other kinds of storms—financial storms or health storms or whatever—it's the exact same thing. For us, we view all of those storms as the opportunity—we have to come together. We don't really have much choice. I quote Shakespeare all the time: "There is no virtue like necessity."[3] But for some of us, we make necessity a joy.

So, the stories that I hear about what my family has—and, you know, those who raised me—what they did in their own time, the story that I didn't say was, there was a threat in my own family in the aftermath of what happened to Emmett Till. My uncle was dealing with a similar situation. What happened was, he was alleged to have whistled at a white girl at the bus station—in the

South. The men threatened my uncle, but they didn't do anything to him. My uncle goes to my grandfather and tells him what happened. He says, "I want you to point them out to me." He put him in his pickup. They drove over to the bus station. He pointed out the men. My grandfather says, "Come with me." He reached in the back of his pickup—right there where people in Texas keep it—and grabbed his rifle. He walked right into the Greyhound station and pointed that rifle at the feet of the people who had threatened his son. He said, "I don't care what you do with these others, but not this one here." That could have killed him. To know that that kind of audacity and tenacity runs in my veins means that I don't need to be afraid of what's here. Also, that which runs from my family's lessons, prepared me for ministry in a season like this.

When I was doing speech and debate, we were competing against UT and several other schools. This girl from UT did her programmed oral interpretation on lynchings, and, like, three or four of the lynchings that she had focused on were in Waco, including Jesse Washington. Because I was in that particular event, I kept being in the room with her and competing throughout that tournament, and it was like torture every single time—like, oh my God, these pictures! Just give her the first place. One of those tournaments was actually at Baylor. She did this presentation that was very anti-Waco in that sense, you know, that old—dredging up the old lynching stories. It was kind of like when I was at Sam Houston and we did *The Exonerated*, which is a play about people who had been sent to death row who were not guilty. It was controversy all over, and people showed up because of the controversy. You know, it was pitch-perfect for the competition.

But I think it also sort of opened my eyes—both, one, to the moment that would come in Huntsville where I would be dealing with that lynching subject, because part of how I got equipped was being in that room. Then, secondly, it would be that—part of what I believe that symbolically did, when at Baylor, was that it made my ear attentive to the stories not that the academics and the historians at Baylor wanted me to know but the stories that the janitors would tell, the stories that the cooks would tell, the stories that the people, the old ladies at the church would tell—whether it be at Antioch Community Church, which I visited, or at Pleasant Olive Missionary Baptist Church when Reverend Monty Francis was there, or where I really loved going, which was Greater New Light with Connie Oliver. These, the rich, long stories—not just of the tornado but of what it was like to strive in Waco—which echoed a lot of what the same story was with my family in other places in Texas as well.

Though I love Baylor and I can sing every word of "That Good Old Baylor Line" to this day, what drew me to those stories was Baylor's hypocrisy. I laid down the fight at Baylor to make them honor MLK's holiday, because they didn't do it before that. That was a travesty, being that he was the only person with a federal holiday in his honor that was a Baptist minister from the South. It wasn't rocket science. That was—and I want to be clear. We fought that fight in 1999. That holiday had been a holiday for two decades. I don't want to get on a soapbox, but I just want to be clear. I think they had honored it in Arizona before they honored it at Baylor. Not good.

It was official hypocrisy that I saw particularly manifested in the upper echelons in the administration at Baylor. It also turned me off so much that I invested a lot of my time, instead of being as a student on campus—though I was probably as invested as any person on campus could have been. I was active in church life. I was active in community life. I volunteered on Mae Jackson's first campaign, when she ran and won for mayor. You know, they actually persuaded me to—I didn't really run, but—to put my name on the ballot for school board in Waco. Mae did. She just wanted somebody to run against the person just so that they wouldn't run unopposed. I was like, "Sure, I'll do it." My first election loss. But I just say that, to say that Waco was that kind of place. The sort of negative energy that you had to work against sometimes when you were, especially as a Black person at Baylor, it made you—in those days, there was not as much diversity at Baylor. For many of us, who had never been away from home for much of a length of time, the only place that we could seek refuge in Waco was in the Black community. So, their stories became our stories.

Well, if there's one thing that, you know, I wouldn't consider the people in Waco, the Black community that I met—and this isn't a negative critique. I wouldn't consider them "effervescent." There's a—oh, my God—W. H. Auden has a long poem. It starts off saying, "Our Father, whose creative Will / Asked Being for us all / Thy word is ever legible, / Thy meaning unequivocal, / And for Thy Goodness even sin / Is valid as a sign." And then he says, "Inflict Thy promises in each / Occasion of distress, / That from our incoherence we / May learn to put our trust in Thee, / And brutal fact persuades us to / Adventure, Art, and Peace."[4] That line is the one that really catches me in that. That's actually a satirical piece, which just blows my mind. But "brutal fact persuades us to Adventure." I think that that's the lesson that I saw embodied in the stories that I was hearing in Waco, that a really dark history informed the id—not necessarily the best part of the people—but the id of the people. Rather than looking through rose-colored lenses, they're hyper-straight with their assessments.

That was something that benefited me. I don't look at a lot of racial matters with a bunch of optimism or rose-colored glasses. I look at it as, this is probably going to be a bloodbath fight to the end, because it's the sin that we just can't seem to repent of. Waco helped me learn that lesson. Whether it be the lessons of Jesse Washington and what happened there. Whether it be some of the challenges Doris Miller faced in his time there. Whether it be—I could go through names and stories. Whether it be in the challenges that had been faced by Paul Quinn campus, that have traced that school from Waco to Dallas and back. All of those things said, there was always this undercurrent of—I hate saying sadness, but there was a sadness. But it wasn't a sadness, like, we've stopped striving. It's just like, it may not get any better. That was sobering for the work that I would do in Waco. But it also—again, it gave me a lens into certain things—like when you're trying to do political activism with people when they feel defeated already. That makes it more hard—more difficult—to get above a certain level. That would be some of the frustration that frequently me and Linda would end up having to talk about and walking through. Like, how not to get despondent because you're dealing with despondent people. The history of Waco did that to a lot of people.

Growing up in the oral tradition in the Black church prepared me, in addition to going to Waco, for receiving, you know—my grandmother—the ethic that we had in the church was—many of our pastors didn't have formal educations. They were divinely inspired, we believed. They preached and they dug. They studied to show themselves approved workmen rightly dividing the word of truth. There was this tendency—like a lot of people—you could have a deacon up there that had a college education, but everybody preferred the one that could really pray. It didn't matter. I think they said, "He got his degree at 'knee bent' college." So, the idea that you could be an authority in our community and not have a title.

Keeping that lesson intact was—it's always been hard going to Baylor or going to any school. But I think that Waco was one of the places where if one was radically open to—and I'll just say Indigenous knowledge. Instead of thinking that everything is in a book, oral history is work that has to be done. It's time-consuming, but it's filled with narratives and stories. I'll just say, the reason why I think that this is important for me is that it's not true just on a sort of social level, interpersonally or intrapersonally. When we go to sleep at night, our bodies tell stories to us, because our minds need to be distracted from the functions that have to happen at sleep. The mind concocts a story and tells it to us. We call them dreams. That's why I said earlier, I think stories are essential. If our body is creating stories for us, maybe we need to understand that, at least at some level—maybe at a spiritual level—the story is important, and the author is not.

What I saw was that an event that lasted a few minutes had a residue that endured generations. The stain of racism, white supremacy, Jim Crow, and good-old-boy Waco politics—I think that toxic mix impressioned itself down to a genetic level on people. It's a trauma. I mean, you can't call it anything else but that. But it was experienced on the physical, on the spiritual, and on the mental—like, you know, your intellect. I don't know why I'm thinking about this. This is—when you were asking the question, my mind was going—so I always will be obedient to, sort of, these ancestral leanings.

When I was a kid—and it's sung all in Waco, Edna, Huntsville, and in the Black church. There was a—I didn't understand it back then. Literally, I was sitting here. It came to me, and I understood it. So, the first part of the song starts off just saying, "Hallelujah, hallelujah, hallelujah. The storm is passing over, hallelujah." The older saints would get so happy about that song: "The storm is passing over, hallelujah." They were ready for the storm to be over with. I get that same ethos about—when they talked about that one and others, they spoke, "We made it." Then, the residue of what it meant. Everybody doesn't look for meaning in the wind. The prophets do. Elijah was hearing the voice of God on a gentle breeze. God in the Bible often is talked about as inhabiting—or at least the Spirit—inhabiting particularly the wind. Whether it be out on the waves, whether it be, you know, wherever. I just think that that is sort of where I was feeling when I was in Waco, that people had that strong sense that whether you believe it to be this or that, it can be this *and* that.

I think that our academic approach to some of these issues or developments—we are trained to think that, in Western thought, it's this or that. The circular understanding of displaced West Africans is, this *and* that. It is circular. Our theologies were circular. Our lives are circular. I think in that understanding—being a part of the Black community—is that they're going to keep this story alive. They're going to remember it and they're going to tell it for generations to come. It will probably have just as much "ooga-booga" in it in fifty years as it does now—because it was never about the facts. This is less about the history. It's *Truth and Method* written by Hans-Georg Gadamer. I think that that is what the story of the tornado is. This is the Black community of Waco developing an "effective history," a history that is meant to link the past to the present, to alter the future. Every sense that I got when I would be engaged by the story in Waco was with a sense that this was an ominous tale that we were telling so that it won't be forgotten, that you won't be caught in the same pathways.

Why is it important to remember Valhalla? Why do we talk about Zeus and Hera? Is it important for us to hear this sort of limited version of history about the Founding Fathers? I think there was value in the tornado story. I really enjoyed *Hamilton* and imagining that people of color could have founded this nation. In some ways, we did. But I just think that the daring to retell the stories, even with their mystical elements—it doesn't make it factual, it makes it human. Because when I tell a joke, I am emotional or deadpan. I think that that's the same way with these relics from our history, particularly from—if we went and told a fact-driven story, that wouldn't be a product of that time. I think that part of what we have to remember when we go back and retell stories—or reread stories or rehear stories—is that stories have lives unto themselves, and they owe allegiance to no one.

Humanity loves to try to control storylines. Storylines tend to buck back against being controlled or manipulated. The story is going to be what it is, especially stories rooted in truth—not *the* truth, but they're rooted in truth. Jokes are also rooted in truth. What's the purpose of the story? That's why I go back to that effective history. The purpose of this story wasn't so much even just the reinstantiation of white supremacy. This story, as is any story told by a faithful people, is for the edification of people. What was edifying in telling that story? That God had not forgotten. That God was watching. God remembers. It might have been translated better for them coming in the form of that story than in some preacher preaching it in a sermon, or some academic talking about it in a lecture. For the people that needed the story, they got what they needed.

The relic that we pass around years and years later, that's a piece of art. Always. What we know of the daily lives of the Greeks, aside from the statues and paintings, it's the theater. They wrote down their thoughts—what they thought society should look like and what was absurd to them and all that. We see in those pieces of art—that is all of the history we really know about these people.

The most complete and thorough vision, and it's the least factual. Most of our history is based off of artistic relics. The least factual things. In fact, I was just watching a thing in that they were talking about cave drawings. They said that the individuals that they were looking at—and now they're making this, this discovery—that a lot of the cave drawings from around the world may have just been drawings of children, just playing because they were bored. Because they could tell from the marks that their hands were of certain sizes, the height of where the things were. Like, these were children. But we've based a lot of history off of the caveman drawings. I just think that the same is true with these stories out of Waco and other places.

I almost forgot where I was. I was about to cuss. But eff Western knowledge. I think that Willie James Jennings—I was reading in, I think it's like *After Whiteness* or something like that.[5] He sort of talks about institutional struggles and the challenges—particularly for the seminary, but for the academy. But it's this idea that we have all kissed this ring for too long. This ring and this institution that we are upholding and preserving has been the death place of my people's stories—the vaunting of understanding that excluded people who looked just like me, and their voices. The people who look just like those Black people in Waco. I think that Margaret Urban Walker argues that we need to establish ourselves as epistemic authorities. We have to be the ones who dictate the story without apology to people—particularly white people—who don't like the way we tell the story.

Look at the whole debate around critical race theory. White people—not you—don't like the way that that story is being told. So, they go back and tell a more complete version of that story. The reaction to it from certain circles is to mute it, to censor it, to stamp it out, to silence it. I think that that is the wrong instinct. The more they try to do that, the more people who are establishing themselves as epistemic authorities have to keep talking, keep telling the story and keep spinning a different narrative. I say "spinning" because it is created and creative.

But I just say that—the expectation would be that I should give the bow to logic. But I think that what is true in my life—and what I have witnessed is true in the lives of people there in the area of Waco—has been that sometimes what happens in life is not logical. And you still have to make meaning out of it. Maybe it's coincidental, but a lot of them preferred it to be providential because they prefer having a God that's on their side. That's important to a people and to a person—that they are not abandoned, they are not forgotten, they are not left on the battlefield to die. Especially after others have already lost their lives unnecessarily, wrongly, like Jesse. In his case, with his story oft repeated—his body drudged up—I think that it becomes important to know that God has something to say about this.

For people who were looking for some answer to theodicy, I think that this story was a part of that process. They had to work out the goodness of God. Even in the one story that I saw where they talked about, like, all the people said, "Oh, we're in this shelter and we're going to be safe." They were not safe. I think that the idea is—logic said that was a safe space, but there are some things that are so much bigger than logic. Much more destructive and powerful than logic. Absurdity is such a thing. I think that we have to fight against that. I think that this story, as—and some people might think it sounded ridiculous—it was a people's battle against absurdity. Whatever words they found to strike the balance, to right the wrongs, to make things a little more level. Frequently in my community, we tell jokes at white people's expense. I'm an honest person. I'm here, talking to a microphone. I'm caught now. But it's less a matter of trying to tear white people down and more trying to figure out a way to let off some of the tension of what's happening in your life. Just laugh about it for a second. Again, we laugh to keep from crying.

I think this story can't be contained for all these years, repeated for all these years, and having permutations all these years—even now, staying hotly debated about its veracity—I think it's important. As important as, you know, the rivalry between the Dallas Cowboys and the Washington Football Team—I don't remember what their new name is. It's an epic, long-standing rivalry. Famed. I think people need those kinds of things. Their mirror neurons want to turn on. They want to cheer for somebody. They want to cheer for their side. I think that this story was a way not to cheer but to encourage. To encourage a people, that a storm may blow, but what comes with that wind is justice. You know, injustice may come once, but also what comes is retribution. The same God of providence is the God of vengeance. The God of love is also the God of accountability. For a people that feels frequently dispossessed, it felt pretty good. Not that people died but that God had something to say about it. God wasn't silent on the story. I think that, for me—and in dwelling in the last few days over some of these subjects and thinking about it both religiously, theologically, historically, as a Black person, sociologically—that's where I land on this, is that. Abraham Joshua Heschel, when he talked about prayer, he says prayer in its best understanding is a song. People need a song, he said. People needed a song.

8

Stevie Walker-Webb

*For Stevie Walker-Webb, to talk about the story of Jesse
Washington is to talk about his grandmother, Lucille Webb:
her voice, her faith, her life, and the transformative influence
these have had on Walker-Webb and so many more.*

My core beliefs—my "who I am"—are a result of being born and
raised in Waco.[1] At eighteen, I moved away to college, just two
hours north in Dallas, where I stayed for about five years. I took
a victory lap getting my undergrad in sociology and political science. Afterward, I moved back to Waco to become the Founding
Artistic Director of the Jubilee Theater for about four and a half
years—that's a whole other story. Most of my life—you know,
I'm thirty-five now—was spent in Waco. I was born in '87, so my
childhood was in the early '90s.

Poverty was so rampant, it became normalized. Despite growing up in and out of public housing, my parents did their best
to shield us from the reality of it. My father, a Marine veteran,
worked long hours, and my mom tried to work part-time, but it
was hard with our large family. Growing up, I didn't understand
how poor we were until I moved to Dallas for college. Later, when
I moved to New York for my master's, my worldview expanded
further. The more I traveled, the more I realized how disadvan-
taged my childhood had been. But back then, I didn't notice
because everyone I knew was poor. Anthropologically, it makes

sense—the neighborhoods I grew up in were victims of white flight, brain drain, and real estate divestment. But as a kid, I didn't know that because everyone around me was in the same boat.

Despite the poverty, I never felt unsafe in my neighborhood. I always felt supported by my community, even though Waco was in the national spotlight in the '90s. I grew up in the shadow of the Branch Davidians, but at five years old, I didn't know what that was. They were on the outskirts of town, yet Waco had this fog, this stain from the incident, compounded by the poverty surrounding us.

I remember coming home from school ravenous, waiting for my mom or grandma to finish cooking. There was a little corner store—no name—two blocks from my grandmother's house. After school, my siblings and I would gather our coins and stop by the store. Back then, you could buy a chimichanga—a deep-fried burrito—for fifty cents. We'd buy three or four, cut them in half, and share. I can still smell the hot, melted bean and cheese filling. We ate them too fast on the walk home, hoping dinner might be more than beans and cornbread—sometimes it was, sometimes it wasn't. But whatever was on the table, the six of us kids ate it with gratitude. Those were the values: sharing, resourcefulness, and finding joy in simple things.

I also remember when the Harry Potter books came out. I was in sixth grade, and we were all bookworms. We could only afford one book at a time, so my mom would take us to Hastings, a video and book store. When we got that first Harry Potter book, I remember standing over my sister Meme's shoulder, reading along because I couldn't wait for her to finish. Meme eventually went to Baylor and now she's doing her PhD in feminist studies and narrative therapy at Texas Women's University. But back then, that book brought us together. Being broke created intimacy among us—it didn't take much for us to see the value in one another.

My grandmother, Lucille Webb, was a huge source of joy. She loved to bake and could make a feast out of crumbs. I don't know how she and my mom fed all of us—plus the cousins and neighborhood kids we'd bring home—but they always did. Our house was "the house." There was a deep sense of community there that I haven't found anywhere since leaving Waco. There was a lot of pain and poverty, but there was also a lot of joy.

Church was both too much and not enough, which is hard to explain. I grew up attending Pentecostal Cathedral of Faith, Church of God in Christ—try saying that five times. It was one of the largest churches in Waco at the time, on East Waco Drive across from G.L. Wiley Middle School. Church was this magical, powerful place that taught me how to be, and at the same time could be a painful, horrible place of condemnation and policing. To this day, I wrestle with questions of self-worth and wonder if God really loves me. On my good days, I know he does.

Black history wasn't taught in schools in Waco, but in my grandmother's house, even Jesus was Black. She had a beautiful picture of a Black Jesus with long dreadlocks in her foyer. My grandmother's stories filled in the gaps left by my formal education. She picked cotton for the first eighteen years of her life, born into the end of the sharecropping era. Her father had been born into slavery, and her grandfather founded one of the first Black Presbyterian churches in Texas, still standing in Elm Mott. The Webbs have a deep historical pride in Waco.

My grandmother used to tell us the story of Jesse Washington. Sometimes on Sundays, we'd drive out to her home church in Elm Mott, which felt like the country back then. She would tell us about how she and her siblings picked cotton there, how the land had been owned by the family that once enslaved her father, and how our family turned that land into a place of worship.

Even though my grandmother wasn't alive when Jesse Washington was lynched, the story was passed down to her, and she passed it down to us. She remembered watching the tornado that later tore through Waco, following the same route they dragged Jesse's body through the streets. To her, and many Black folks in Waco, that tornado was seen as God's retribution.

For a long time, Waco's downtown bore the scars of that tornado. I remember seeing a plastic straw embedded in a brick wall, thinking it was a relic of the tornado's force. Maybe someone just stuck it there, but in my child's mind, it was a reminder of the devastation that had lingered for decades.

Waco had been poised to be a major city, but the tornado halted those plans. Many Black folks, myself included, believe it was God's way of getting justice—not just for Jesse Washington, but for generations of Black people who suffered under racism, segregation, and the legacy of slavery.

I grew up with an awareness that the veil between the living and the dead was thin, and that the distance between past and present was just a story. We were raised on stories of survival and self-determination. My grandmother, my mom, and my dad never allowed us to call ourselves poor. Even when we were living with my grandmother, they wouldn't let us use that word.

At one point, when Waco ISD had strict zoning rules, my mom fabricated our address so we could attend Dean Highland Elementary, which was supposed to be a better school than the one in our neighborhood. I remember being called the "stinky kid" there by the other children. I didn't realize at the time that they were calling me poor.

Whenever I complained about being bullied, my grandmother would tell me stories about Jesse Washington or her own childhood. She always put my little grievances into the larger context of history and struggle, reminding me that the world was bigger than my immediate problems. It was her way of acknowledging my pain while giving me a broader perspective. "At once, yes, you are oppressed," she'd say, "but also, forgive them—they know not what they do."

Madea—that's what we called her—would tell us stories from her childhood, stories of survival, to help us face our own struggles. After these conversations, I always felt better, not just because of her attention but because I left with a deep sense of pride. I was being raised by a woman who, despite facing the impossible, remained undefeated. Her strength, her blood, her love—they still flow in my veins. Whenever I think of my grandmother, I think of my responsibility and my ability to create change, no matter how much things in Waco have or haven't changed.

It was 1991 or '92, and I was just a kid—five, maybe seven—when my grandmother told me about Jesse Washington, something that happened way back in 1916. That year always struck me as cosmic, almost a palindrome with 1619, the year the first enslaved Black person was brought to this continent. From 1619 to 1916, to 1991, here was my grandmother still telling the story of a brutal lynching, illustrating how depraved and inhuman white supremacy could be.

But she never told these stories to vilify white people. It wasn't about stirring rage, though God knows that would've been a fair response. No, her stories were meant to equip us, to help us understand the world we were navigating. She would tell us about injustice, microaggressions from teachers because we were poor and Black, or getting pulled over by the police for no reason. But she'd always say, "Let the Lord fight your battle." Her approach wasn't about rage or bitterness but about knowing which battles were hers to fight and which she could leave to God. People today might call that pacifism, but Madea was no pushover. She was made of love and gristle, a woman who survived Jim Crow, segregation, and being born a sharecropper, and went on to become a business owner and homeowner, integrating her neighborhood when she moved west of the Brazos River.

She had grit and tenacity, and she wasn't afraid to show us the horrors of life. But she also didn't want to burden us with bitterness. I don't know how she did it, how she survived so much while keeping her light intact. My grandmother knew that the most important fight was within, that liberation is as much an internal battle as an external one. The story of Jesse Washington was just one of many. She had lived through deeply personal traumas but managed to walk through fire without smelling of smoke, without becoming bitter or small. She passed on the truth of life while showing us the power of love.

Growing up, I preferred Madea's vibrant, unfiltered version of history to the watered-down lies in school textbooks. Her stories were full of people with names and faces, people who loved and resisted as much as they struggled. They were aware of their place in society, aware of the unjust cards dealt to them, but they persisted, their eyes on a future they might never see, hoping to manifest it for their descendants.

I always say that my grandmother's stories are my inheritance. They are the most precious thing she left me, giving me an unshakable sense of who I am. I remember in school, getting in trouble because a teacher claimed slavery ended with the Emancipation Proclamation. But even at twelve, I knew about Juneteenth, about how not everyone in Texas was free in 1865. It was 1998 or something, and Juneteenth wasn't celebrated nationally, not even in Texas. I got in trouble for trying to correct the historical record, because staying quiet felt like a betrayal of my grandmother's truth, and that could not be.

For me, my grandmother has always been holy, and her stories sacred. If 1865 really meant freedom for all, then it would mean my ancestors were liars. And at twelve, I couldn't stomach that. So if it came down to Honest Abe or Holy Ghost–filled Lucille Webb, I was putting my faith in Madea every time. The tragedy of history told from a white, imperialistic framework is that you only get half the truth. Accepting that means accepting that your ancestors, or their narratives, were built on lies. That's a terrible burden to bear, and I felt it even as a child.

I was that kid—the one too excited about Black History Month. While my Black friends groaned, I was fired up. Every year, I made sure my teachers caught hell in February because I needed them to tell the whole story. They would talk about slavery without addressing the lives and personhood of my people. But I could tell them what my people were really like, raised by someone who had lived through sharecropping.

The first time I talked about Jesse Washington in school, I got in trouble. We were in the middle of a tornado drill, and the sirens were going off, but I started talking about Jesse. My grandmother always told the story when it stormed. It became something I carried to school with me, even though it got me in trouble.

This story meant so much to my grandmother because it showed her that God cared about her, a poor Black girl born a sharecropper who picked cotton for the first eighteen years of her life. For her, the story of Jesse Washington wasn't just about horror—it was about justice, about the belief that God had her back. My grandmother lived through that history, and while many white people did too, I often wonder how they pass those stories down. Do they tell their children what it was like to witness a lynching, or do they bury it? You can't forget something like that.

I think my grandmother held on to the story of Jesse Washington because to her, it was one of those rare moments when cosmic righteousness showed up in the real world. In our religious society, God is often weaponized by the powerful, used to justify all kinds of brutality. But the connection Black people in Waco made between Jesse's lynching in 1916 and the tornado of 1953 was different—it was a sign that God was on our side, if only for a moment.

I don't think my grandmother would've said it like that, but she always told us, "God has the final say." It was her way of saying, "God's got our back." Her favorite scripture, which I now have tattooed on my chest, was, "Touch not mine anointed and do my prophets no harm." When the city of Waco finally reckons with its history and memorializes Jesse Washington, I hope they inscribe that scripture on his monument.

Growing up, my family went to church several times a week. Our pastor was politically savvy and always tied his sermons to the struggles of Black Wacoans, though he never preached about Jesse Washington. That always struck me as strange, given the mystical tradition of the Church of God in Christ—people who believed in the power of touch, of laying hands, of call and response. Magic. And yet, no one sermonized about Jesse. Maybe the connection between faith, systemic racism, and the supernatural was too much for the pulpit.

To this day, if you Google "Jesse Washington" or "Waco Horror," you'll find images of his charred, dehumanized body. The ghosts of slavery and Jim Crow are still with us, not just in black-and-white photos but in the very fabric of our society—in the street names, in the parks, in the city's real estate.

I can't look at Magnolia Silos without thinking about slavery, about the history of sugarcane and the continued divestment in certain Waco communities. Poor people are being pushed to the edges of the city. The racial attitudes that allowed Jesse Washington's lynching in 1916 echo through time, through the gentrification that is displacing Black and poor folks today.

The story of Jesse Washington hasn't been told enough. If it were, if the city of Waco were to truly reckon with its past, maybe it could improve race relations, or lead to more investment in neglected communities. Jesse's life had meaning, and it's up to us to make something meaningful out of the tragedy of his death. But we can't do that if we don't tell the story.

I wonder why his story isn't in the schoolbooks, at least in Waco. Who benefits from the silence? When I think about historical markers, I think about those small, barely noticeable plaques. That's not enough. And this isn't about PTSD. I wasn't there; I didn't see it. But because we haven't learned from it, history keeps repeating itself. Jesse Washington, Emmett Till, Eric Garner, Sandra Bland—how can we forget? And yet, somehow, we do. Who wins when we forget?

That's what makes me sad about Waco. When I look at the Silos, and I see wealthy white people displacing the poor, or Baylor University expanding while poor people lose their homes, I think about Jesse Washington. The same forces at work then are still at work today.

Epilogue
The Spirit of the Whirlwind

The stories of Black Wacoans have the potential to shape new ways of living in the uneven landscape of Central Texas. To take these stories seriously is to recognize oneself as a neighbor to the storytelling community and its tradition of social justice theory and praxis. In the local context, this means receiving stories like those gathered in *God of the Whirlwind* as a collective invitation to become neighbors through listening, solidarity, and action.

Like prophecies, stories refuse domestication. Even local stories, like the whirlwind story, whose significance may seem confined to only one time and place, find new meaning when they are told elsewhere. Distant listeners generate new insights, making connections between the story and their own lives. In addition to challenging the arrangements of power in their immediate context, then, stories from below may also inspire new ways of seeing and acting in faraway times and places. I have come to think of the capacity of the whirlwind story to inspire imagination and action in settings beyond its origin in terms of its spirit.

It should not be taken for granted that the retelling of the whirlwind story preserves community and historical memories of Black Waco: Jesse Washington, lynch law, the tornado, and powerful community interventions to hold Washington and others in memory while challenging the dominance of plantation lynch law by telling prophetic weather tales. And yet, of special concern is that, beyond the powers of preservation, the whirlwind story does something more: it carries a productive force, a spirit, which elicits distinct ways of seeing and acting in the world.

This spirit has appeared in stories throughout *God of the Whirlwind*. In Stevie Walker-Webb's contribution, it appears in the active call to overcome the "racial attitudes that allowed Jesse Washington's lynching in 1916" and are manifested in "the gentrification that is displacing Black and poor folks today." This call entails building a shareable world where all are able to live dignified lives. Beyond the chapters of this book, the spirit is also manifest in the struggle against the horror of capital punishment, the toxic residue of lynch law which continues to misconstrue justice as retribution. It is worth recalling that if the white Waco mob had not seized Washington in the frenzied courtroom and lynched him, he would have been legally—and no less unjustly—hanged according to Texas law under the direction of the sheriff. Waco native Rickey Cummings gives voice to something like the spirit of the whirlwind in his deeply humane account of practicing vigil on Texas's death row—a holding in heart and mind of friends and himself as they seek to survive and advance an abolitionist vision of justice.[1]

These examples of the spirit of the whirlwind—its contemporary challenge to the injustices of political economy and capital punishment—represent two potential scenes for discernment. The larger aspiration of *God of the Whirlwind* remains that, in hearing this and other stories from Black Waco, readers will be moved to receive in their own contexts the community knowledge, memories, and stories from below needed for re-creating common life.

Acknowledgments

I wish to express my deepest gratitude to participating narrators whose collaboration made this project possible: Reverend Michael Babers, Bettie Beard, Ramad Carter, LaRue Dorsey, Anthony Fulbright, Nona Kirkpatrick, Linda Jann Lewis, Reverend George Oliver, and Stevie Walker-Webb. I'm grateful to them for sharing their time, memories, and stories and also for continuing to answer my phone calls. I am additionally grateful to many other Wacoans who encouraged and inspired the project along the way. This book is the result of a long and life-giving conversation with the brilliant Stevie Walker-Webb, going back to the first time he shared with me the story of the whirlwind that his grandmother Lucille Webb shared with him. The book would have been unimaginable apart from him.

Research funding support through a Fellows Grant from The Crossroads Project, a collaborative research initiative codirected by Anthea Butler, Lerone Martin, and Judith Weisenfeld, based at Princeton University and supported by the Henry Luce Foundation, helped bring this project to fruition. Judith Weisenfeld went above and beyond in shepherding an earlier presentation of some of these materials during my fellowship. Her continued support has been indispensable. Many thanks are due to Michelle Holland, Stephen Sloan, and all the staff of the Baylor University Institute for Oral History for providing transcription services, a repository for housing the full-length version of the interviews, and guidance in navigating the complex work of oral history; and to Joseph Winters, Paul Martens, and Natalie Carnes, who also generously supported my dissertation research, which informed the backdrop to this project. I'm grateful to have been able to work with

Dave Nelson, Jenny Hunt, and the whole team at Baylor University Press, who received this project and patiently fostered its development and completion.

My research for this book received additional material support at different stages from the Charlotte W. Newcombe Foundation, Political Theology Network, Baylor University's Department of Religion, and St. Mary's University's Department of Theology. More broadly, my work has benefited from being surrounded by a tremendous community of committed scholars, students, and staff at St. Mary's University, including Margaret Cantú-Sánchez, Irene Holguin, Jason King, Ivan Morales, Gerald Poyo, Belinda Román, Sara Ronis, Stella Silva, Betsy Smith, Isabella Vasquez, and Veronica Villela-Perez, in addition to other colleagues in the Program in Mexican American Studies, Department of Theology, Center for Catholic Studies, and SPARC Office.

This book was deeply shaped by collaboration with Mark Menjívar, whose creative practice and technical knowledge enhanced all its dimensions—especially the addition of visual elements. Matt Harris, Emily Phillips Davis, Heath Pearson, Ry Siggelkow, and Jonathan Tran helped me envision the project from the beginning—encouraging, caring for, and contributing to its making in countless ways. Ramad Carter helped me see its potential value early on. Thomas Breedlove shared timely and needed words. Nyle Fort, Carl Hughes, Jason King, Nathan Maddox, and Will Wellman improved everything through responses to drafts. Reverend George Oliver relayed important resources for the introduction, and Natalia Montemayor facilitated space for its completion. Brady Beard, Malcolm Foley, Tom Millay, and J. P. O'Connor encouraged this project through conversation. I'm grateful to each of them.

My big sister, Abby Heitshusen, shaped this book in more ways than I'm able to name. I'm grateful to my parents, Robert and Lori Davis, for their love and support and for sparking my imagination in the elements at the heart of this book. And in memory of my grandparents, William and Marie Faber, and Don and Joan Davis, for their love. My last gratitude is to Emily, Esme, and Maya for their loving accompaniment in the making of this book.

Note on Editing Practices
and Interviews

The chapters in this book draw from full-length oral history interviews, which were conducted during the summer of 2022 with the support of a research fellowship with The Crossroads Project and are now preserved at the Baylor University Institute for Oral History. They have been changed from the dialogical format of the oral history interview to the monologue chapter format. Additionally, each interview was edited for thematic purposes and to facilitate readability while striving to preserve, as far as possible, their original dialogical quality. This editing process entailed ongoing collaboration with narrators, who reviewed the chapters and made any additional edits prior to publication. Minimal insertions in brackets and endnotes have been added for clarification.

Mark Menjívar provided support for two of the interviews, as indicated in chapter endnotes. The narrators reflect relative generational diversity and consist of Black women and men who are retired and active educators, disaster relief workers, artists, activists, community organizers, ministers, and local leaders. Many have lived in Waco for decades; all are in some way deeply connected to the city and to Central Texas even if they no longer reside there. Interviews were conducted in a number of environments, including a living room in East Waco, the East Waco Public Library, the lunch buffet at the Baylor Club, the recording studio of the Institute for Oral History, and Mount Sinai Missionary Baptist Church in San Antonio, Texas. Two were conducted over Zoom.

Notes

Introduction

1 Events leading up to the lynching, and the lynching itself, are not recounted here. For accounts of the event, see W. E. B. Du Bois, "The Waco Horror," Supplement, *The Crisis*, no. 12 (1916): 1–8; James M. SoRelle, "The 'Waco Horror': The Lynching of Jesse Washington," *Southwestern Historical Quarterly* 86, no. 4 (1983): 517–36; William D. Carrigan, *The Making of a Lynching Culture: Violence and Vigilantism in Central Texas, 1836–1916* (Urbana: University of Illinois Press, 2004); Patricia Bernstein, *The First Waco Horror: The Lynching of Jesse Washington and the Rise of the NAACP* (College Station: Texas A&M University Press, 2005); Amy Louise Wood, *Lynching and Spectacle: Witnessing Racial Violence in America, 1890–1940* (Chapel Hill: University of North Carolina Press, 2011); Terry Anne Scott, *Lynching and Leisure: Race and the Transformation of Mob Violence in Texas* (Fayetteville: University of Arkansas Press, 2022); Mari N. Crabtree, *My Soul Is a Witness: The Traumatic Afterlife of Lynching* (New Haven: Yale University Press, 2023). On the "legend of safety," which began with Spanish conquistador Francisco Vázquez de Coronado, see John Edward Weems, *The Tornado* (College Station: Texas A&M University Press, 1991 [1977]), 73–88. The property damage caused by the 1953 tornado is estimated at around $51 million. Memories of the terrible storm persist to this day through the stories of Waco residents, the scars left on downtown structures, and public memorials.

2 Mary Denkins, interviewed by William Carrigan, January 11, 1994, in Waco, Texas. Compact disc. Available at the Baylor University Institute for Oral History.

3 Rosemarie Freeney Harding, *Remnants: A Memoir of Spirit, Activism, and Mothering*, with Rachel Elizabeth Harding (Durham, N.C.: Duke University Press, 2015), 20. Given its preservation across generations, the whirlwind story is a powerful example of the *success* of memory, a reality which is in need of deliberate and systematic attention, as Karen Fields has compellingly argued. See Fields, "What One Cannot Remember Mistakenly," *Oral History* 17, no. 1, Health and Caring (1989): 44–53. For similar examples, see Angela D. Sims, *Lynched: The Power of Memory in a Culture of Terror* (Waco, Tex: Baylor University Press, 2016).

4 Numerous texts could be cited as representative of Texana establishment history. Yet even among other influential texts in this category, it would be difficult to find a better representative than T. R. Fehrenbach's *Lone Star: A History of Texas and the Texans* (Boston: Da Capo Press, 2000 [1968]). The distinction between stories and boasts and the account of the power of stories is informed by John Berger's discussion of stories in his "Ten Dispatches about Endurance in Face of Walls." See Berger, *Hold Everything Dear: Dispatches on Survival and Resistance* (New York: Vintage International, 2008), 98–102.

5 For representative examples of works challenging establishment Texas history and mythmaking, see Annette Gordon-Reed, *On Juneteenth* (New York: Liveright, 2021), especially 97–117; Bryan Burrough, Chris Tomlinson, and Jason Stanford, *Forget the Alamo: The Rise and Fall of an American Myth* (New York: Penguin Press, 2021); Jessica Goudeau, *We Were Illegal: Uncovering a Texas Family's Mythmaking and Migration* (New York: Viking, 2024). Gerald Horne has also recently written an extended counter to establishment histories, arguing that the features I characterize as rooted in the plantation are in fact the basis for larger patterns of fascism in the United States. See Horne, *The Counter-revolution of 1836: Texas Slavery & Jim Crow and the Roots of U.S. Fascism* (New York: International Publishers, 2022). The passage cited comes from Gordon-Reed, *On Juneteenth*, 107. The critical intervention of history "from below" has a rich and varied genealogy. For paradigmatic examples, see Peter Linebaugh and Marcus Rediker, *The Many-Headed Hydra: Sailors, Slaves, Commoners, and the Hidden History of the Revolutionary Atlantic* (Boston: Beacon

Press, 2000); E. P. Thompson, *Witness against the Beast: William Blake and the Moral Law* (New York: New Press, 1993); and, more recently, see the graphic novel project of the migrant justice organization Pueblos de Lucha y Esperanza, "Unshackling Freedom" (2024).

6 For previous engagement with the whirlwind story, see Tyler B. Davis, "The Whirlwind and the Lynching Tree: Apocalyptic and Liberation Theology in the Black Waco Tradition" (PhD diss., Baylor University, 2021). A digital presentation, including audio recordings, was created as part of Princeton University's Crossroads Project. See Tyler B. Davis, "God of the Whirlwind: An Archive of a Black Waco Oral Tradition," *SPIRIT HOUSE: The Crossroads Project*, October 2023, https://www.crossroads-spirithouse.org/davis. As one example of providential interpretation, Alexander Gordon—a white Presbyterian minister from Scotland who involved himself in the abolitionist movement in rural New York—spoke of providence in the explosion aboard the USS Princeton on February 28, 1844. This event caused major setbacks in the pro-slavery effort to annex Texas, Gordon discerned nothing less than God's "terrible work in righteousness" intended to prompt the North into alignment with the abolitionist cause. See Alexander Gordon, *Memoir of Rev. Alexander Gordon: Pastor of the Associate Presbyterian Church, Johnstown, Fulton County, New York*, comp. Amanda Miller (Philadelphia: William S. Young, 1846), 158.

7 Vincent Harding, *There Is a River: The Black Struggle for Freedom in America* (New York: Harcourt Brace & Company, 1981), xii. The language of "spiritual despotism" is drawn from Alexis de Tocqueville as quoted in Clyde Woods, *Development Arrested: The Blues and Plantation Power in the Mississippi Delta* (New York: Verso, 2017 [1998]), 54. On the search for meaning, see Harding, *There Is a River*, xi–xiii.

8 That lynching was a feature, not an anomaly, of the social order echoes Ida B. Wells-Barnett's analysis of lynching as an "unwritten law" in the United States. See, especially, Ida B. Wells-Barnett, "Lynch Law in America," in *The Light of Truth: Writings of an Anti-Lynching Crusader*, ed. Mia Bay and Henry Louis Gates Jr. (New York: Penguin, 2014 [1900]), 394. On African American theological traditions linking the lynching tree to the cross of Jesus Christ, see, especially, James H. Cone, *The Cross and the Lynching Tree* (Maryknoll, N.Y.: Orbis Books, 2011). Ascribing religious and theological importance to tornado phenomena in the North American context has a

surprisingly dynamic history. On this, see Peter J. Thuesen, *Tornado God: American Religion and Violent Weather* (New York: Oxford University Press, 2020). Monica M. Martinez has identified a similar tornado oral tradition in Rocksprings, Texas, emerging in the aftermath of the lynching of Antonio Rodríguez. See Martinez, *The Injustice Never Leaves You: Anti-Mexican Violence in Texas* (Cambridge, Mass.: Harvard University Press, 2018).

9 As Clyde Woods has written, the plantation aimed for total institutional monopoly of all aspects of life. It sought to be town, home, workplace, lumbermill, ranch, farm, recreational area, religious grounds, prison, and cemetery. See Woods, *Development Arrested*, especially 4–12, 48–49, 95–103. On Texas as a borderland plantation society, see Sean M. Kelley, *Los Brazos de Dios: A Plantation Society in the Texas Borderlands, 1821–1865* (Baton Rouge: Louisiana State University Press, 2010), 5; Andrew J. Torget, *Seeds of Empire: Cotton, Slavery, and the Transformation of the Texas Borderlands, 1800–1850* (Chapel Hill: University of North Carolina Press, 2018). For a recounting of the perilous effects of plantation slavery on Black women as well as practices of opposition, see Daina Ramey Berry and Kali Nicole Gross, *A Black Women's History of the United States: ReVisioning American History* (Boston: Beacon Press, 2020), 69–71, etc. For an important example of Black women's opposition to racial slavery with parallels to the Black Waco whirlwind story, see the reconstruction of how Black women transmitted counter-memories and stories of the death of Nat Turner to contest dominant historical memory in Adam Thomas, "The Many Deaths of Nat Turner: Contested Historical Memory under Slavery and Segregation," *Journal of Southern History* 90, no. 1 (2024): 5–44.

10 Randolph B. Campbell, *An Empire for Slavery: The Peculiar Institution in Texas, 1821–1865* (Baton Rouge: Louisiana State University Press, 1991), 84. These numbers reflect the population in 1860. Neil Foley regards Central Texas as "the cultural core" and "ethnoracial borderlands" of the state, given the demographic and cultural collisions occurring under the economic conditions of the agrarian empire. See Foley, *The White Scourge: Mexicans, Blacks, and Poor Whites in Texas Cotton Culture* (Berkeley: University of California Press, 1999), 15; Campbell, *Empire for Slavery*, 274–76; Art Leatherwood, "Stroud, Logan Almaren," Texas State Historical Association, accessed June 2, 2024, https://www.tshaonline.org/handbook/entries/stroud-logan-almaren. These numbers follow Campbell's

documentation. Neely Tucker estimates that the Logan Stroud Plantation held "more than 150" enslaved persons. See Neely Tucker, "The Birth of Juneteenth; Voices of the Enslaved," *Library of Congress Blog*, June 19, 2020, accessed June 2, 2024, https://blogs .loc.gov/teachers/2020/06/the-birth-of-juneteenth-voices-of-the -enslaved/. The scene from Juneteenth at the Stroud Plantation is also drawn from Tucker, "The Birth of Juneteenth," at the insightful direction of Reverend George Oliver.

11 The reflection from an early settler is quoted in Weems, *Tornado*, 80. Jim Stingley, "The Texas Cotton Palace," *Waco History*, accessed June 2, 2024, https://wacohistory.org/items/show/15.

12 Postwar demographic shifts in Waco are helpfully summarized in Alex Hoffman, "The Kinetic South," *Southern Cultures* 27, no. 2 (2021): 62–83, https://www.southerncultures.org/article/the-kinetic -south/. The summary of the effects of plantation society is informed by Woods, *Development Arrested*, as well as Torget, *Seeds of Empire*.

13 This section draws from John Berger's careful analysis of peasant class and culture. See Berger, *Pig Earth* (New York: Vintage Books, 1992 [1979]) xii–xiv. Historians since W. E. B. Du Bois have tracked the way that violence in Texas was a critical strategy for overthrowing state Reconstruction efforts and reestablishing planter economic and political power. See, especially, Du Bois, *Black Reconstruction in America, 1860–1880* (New York: Free Press, 1992 [1935]), 553–61.

14 Equal Justice Initiative's report documents racial terror lynchings between 1877 and 1950. Equal Justice Initiative, "Lynching in America: Confronting the Legacy of Racial Terror, Third Edition," accessed June 11, 2024, https://lynchinginamerica.eji.org/report/. On lynching violence against Black women, see Crystal Feimster, *Southern Horrors: Women and the Politics of Rape and Lynching* (Cambridge, Mass.: Harvard University Press, 2009), 159. See also Julie Buckner Armstrong, *Mary Turner and the Memory of Lynching* (Athens: University of Georgia Press, 2011). On Central Texas numbers, see Carrigan, *Making of a Lynching Culture*, 113–14.

15 Although not focusing on Waco, Keeanga-Yamahtta Taylor's *Race for Profit* identifies sweeping national patterns of predatory inclusion for would-be African American homeowners after the Fair Housing Act and other civil rights legislation. See Taylor, *Race for Profit: How Banks and the Real Estate Industry Undermine Black Homeownership* (Chapel Hill: University of North Carolina Press, 2019). Robert Perkinson elaborates the Texas "punishment business" in detail. See

Perkinson, *Texas Tough: The Rise of America's Prison Empire* (New York: Picador, 2010), 4. A number of historical studies, especially in lynching scholarship, give attention to the entangled relationship between legal and extralegal killing, the death penalty and lynching. See, for one example, Michael J. Pfeifer, *Rough Justice: Lynching and American Society, 1874–1947* (Urbana: University of Illinois Press, 2004). Pfeifer writes, "capital punishment in the United States carries the profound legacy of lynching . . . The arbitrary, racialized, and performative characteristics of today's death penalty carry on what was most important to the advocates of rough justice: that the guilt, innocence, or humanity of an executed person matter less than the collective vengeance satisfied by the ritualized taking of their life" (153). Recent quantitative studies have further underscored a connection. See, for instance, Frank R. Baumgartner, Christian Caron, and Scott Duxbury, "Racial Resentment and the Death Penalty," *Journal of Race, Ethnicity, and Politics* 8, no. 1 (2023): 42–60, https://doi.org/10.1017/rep.2022.30. As of late spring 2024, there are 180 people on death row in Texas. According to the Texas Department of Criminal Justice, 83 are Black. Death row statistics are available through the Texas Department of Criminal Justice. See "Gender and Racial Statistics of Death Row Inmates," Texas Department of Criminal Justice, accessed June 4, 2024, https://www.tdcj.texas.gov/death_row/dr_gender_racial_stats.html.

16 See Linda Jann Lewis's chapter, p. 41.

17 For analysis of Price's recollection, see Adam Gussow, *Seems Like Murder Here: Southern Violence and the Blues Tradition* (Chicago: University of Chicago Press, 2002), 59–65; see also Carrigan, *Making of a Lynching Culture*, 201–2; Sammy Price, *What Do They Want? A Jazz Autobiography*, ed. Caroline Richmond (Oxford: Bayou Press, 1989), esp. 1–14. Stevie Walker-Webb recounts his grandmother Lucille Webb's storytelling in his chapter. On the struggle over the courthouse mural, see Armando Villafranca, "Controversy Born over Courthouse Mural," *Houston Chronicle*, June 30, 2002, https://www.chron.com/news/houston-texas/article/Controversy-born-over-courthouse-mural-2062959.php. The contested murals are pictured on pp. 16–17. For coverage of the public debut of the Texas historical marker about the lynching of Jesse Washington, see Will Bostwick, "Inside the Decades-Long Effort to Commemorate a Notorious Waco Lynching," *Texas Monthly*, February 23, 2023, https://www

.texasmonthly.com/being-texan/waco-historical-marker-saga-jesse
-washington-lynching/. Rickey D. Cummings Jr. offers this and other
powerful reflections in his book with Mark Menjívar, *Holding Vigil*
(Thick Press, 2022), 19. The forthcoming anti-lynching theological
pamphlet by Waco-based pastor and historian Malcolm Foley might
also be added to these. See Foley, *The Anti-Greed Gospel: Why the
Love of Money Is the Root of Racism and How the Church Can Create
a New Way Forward* (Grand Rapids: Brazos Press, 2025).

18 Nona Kirkpatrick's family story is also referred to in Bernstein, *First
Waco Horror*, 25–26.

19 Berger, *Hold Everything Dear*, 102. Understanding Black Waco narrators in terms of organic intellectuals reflects Clyde Woods's reca-
libration of the sites from where knowledge and theory are valued.
Woods writes, "The privileging of indigenous knowledge, of blues
epistemology, and of millions of organic intellectuals denies power to
another elite-led regime of stagnation. What is left? A society where
every member is both a teacher and a student." Woods, *Development
Arrested*, 290.

1 LaRue Dorsey

1 Interviewed on June 28, 2022, in Dorsey's home in East Waco.

2 Linda Jann Lewis

1 Interviewed on June 29, 2022, in Lewis's home in East Waco.

2 The plantations owned by L. M. Stroud of Freestone County and
L. A. Stroud of Limestone County were two of the largest in the state
of Texas, enslaving approximately 212 people in 1860. L. A. Stroud
and his wife also managed an estate that had seventy enslaved people.
See Campbell, *Empire for Slavery*, 275–76.

3 Daryl Janes and Jesse Jackson, *No Apologies: Texas Radicals Celebrate
the '60s* (Austin: Eakin Press, 1992).

3 Michael D. Babers

1 Interviewed on August 26, 2022, via Zoom in San Antonio, Texas.

2 Bernstein, *First Waco Horror*.

4 Bettie V. Beard

1 Interviewed by Tyler B. Davis and Mark Menjívar on June 15, 2022,
at the Baylor Club in Waco, Texas.

2 The Gem Theatre was an African American theater, reflecting the Jim Crow standards of segregation.

5 Nona Kirkpatrick and Anthony Fulbright

1 Interviewed on June 16, 2022, at the East Waco Library.
2 Referring to the lynching of Jesse Washington.
3 The Raleigh Hotel building is still located on Eighth Street and Austin Avenue but is no longer a hotel.
4 Fulbright is referring to the origin of the story linking the tornado to Sank Majors or Jesse Washington.
5 Fulbright quotes from *Rubáiyát of Omar Khayyám*.
6 Fulbright quotes from Psalm 121:1-2.
7 Kirkpatrick is reflecting on whether she believes the tornado was God's justice.
8 Kirkpatrick is referring to the shooting that occurred at Twenty-First Street and Maize Road in Wichita, Kansas, on February 10, 2022.

6 Ramad D. Carter

1 Interviewed by Tyler B. Davis and Mark Menjívar on June 14, 2022, at the recording studio of the Baylor University Institute for Oral History.

7 George Oliver

1 Interviewed on July 28, 2022, at Mt. Sinai Missionary Baptist Church in San Antonio, Texas.
2 Mark 4:39.
3 Oliver is quoting from *Richard II*.
4 Oliver is quoting from "The Summons" in W. H. Auden's *For the Time Being: A Christmas Oratorio*.
5 Willie James Jennings, *After Whiteness: An Education in Belonging* (Grand Rapids: Eerdmans, 2020).

8 Stevie Walker-Webb

1 Interviewed on August 24, 2022, via Zoom in San Antonio, Texas.

Epilogue

1 Stevie Walker-Webb, p. 138; Cummings, with Mark Menjívar, *Holding Vigil*.

www.ingramcontent.com/pod-product-compliance
Lightning Source LLC
Chambersburg PA
CBHW062323040225
21453CB00009B/212